Blank Guitar Tablature and Manusc

Chord Grids

Published by **www.fundamental-changes.com**

ISBN: 978-1505785494

www.fundamental-changes.com

Also By Fundamental-Changes.com

Fundamental Changes in Jazz Guitar I: The Major ii V I for Bebop Guitar

Minor ii V Mastery for Jazz Guitar

Jazz Blues Soloing for Guitar

Guitar Scales in Context

Drop 2 Chord Voicings for Jazz and Modern Guitar

The CAGED System and 100 Licks for Blues Guitar

The Complete Guide to Playing Blues Guitar Book One: Rhythm Guitar

The Complete Guide to Playing Blues Guitar Book Two: Melodic Phrasing

The Complete Guide to Playing Blues Guitar Book Three: Beyond Pentatonics

The Complete Guide to Playing Blues Guitar Compilation (Paperback)

The Complete Technique, Theory and Scales Compilation for Guitar (Paperback)

Sight Reading Mastery for Guitar

Complete Technique for Modern Guitar

Rock Guitar Un-CAGED: The CAGED System and 100 Licks for Rock Guitar

Jazz Guitar Chord Mastery

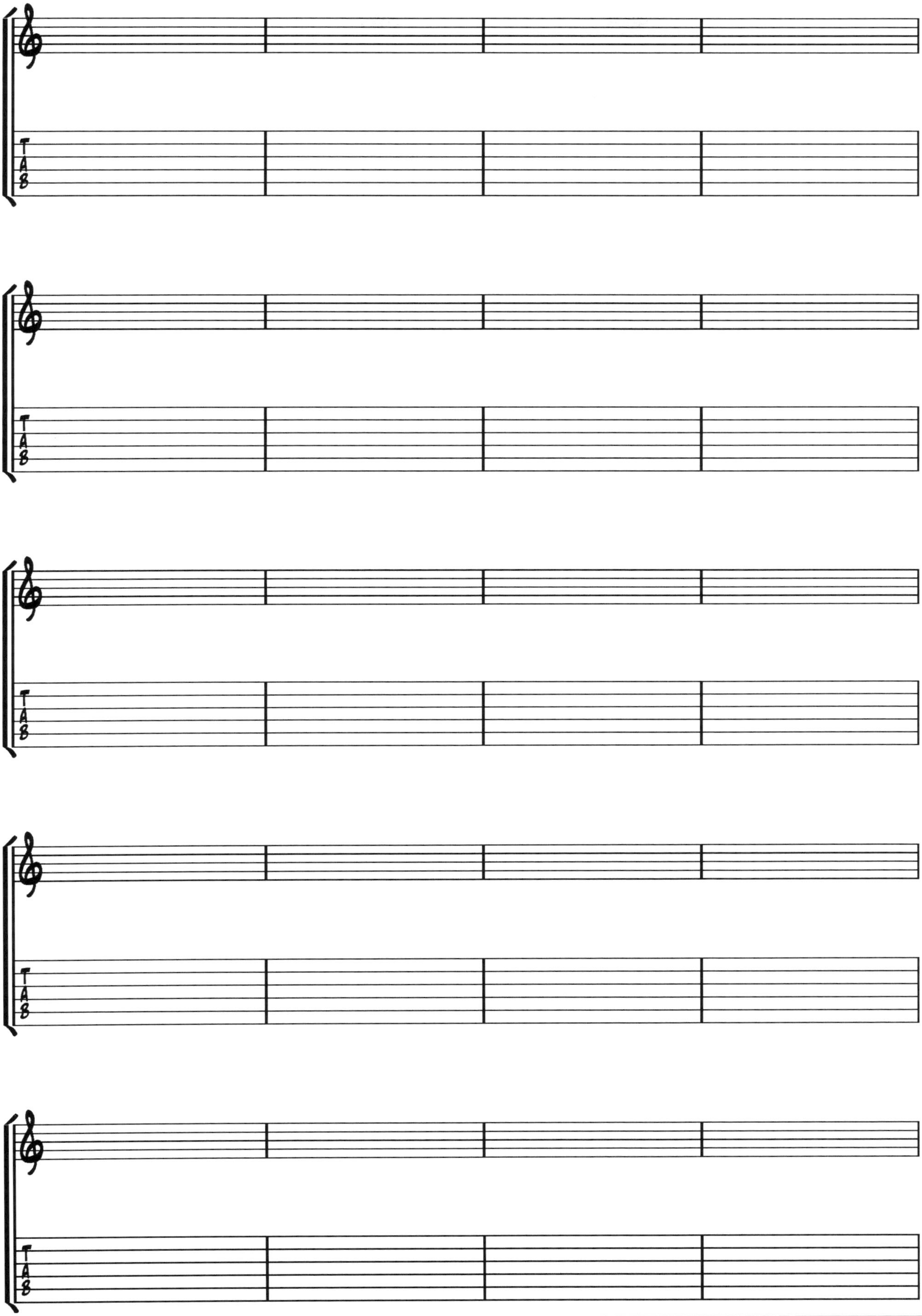

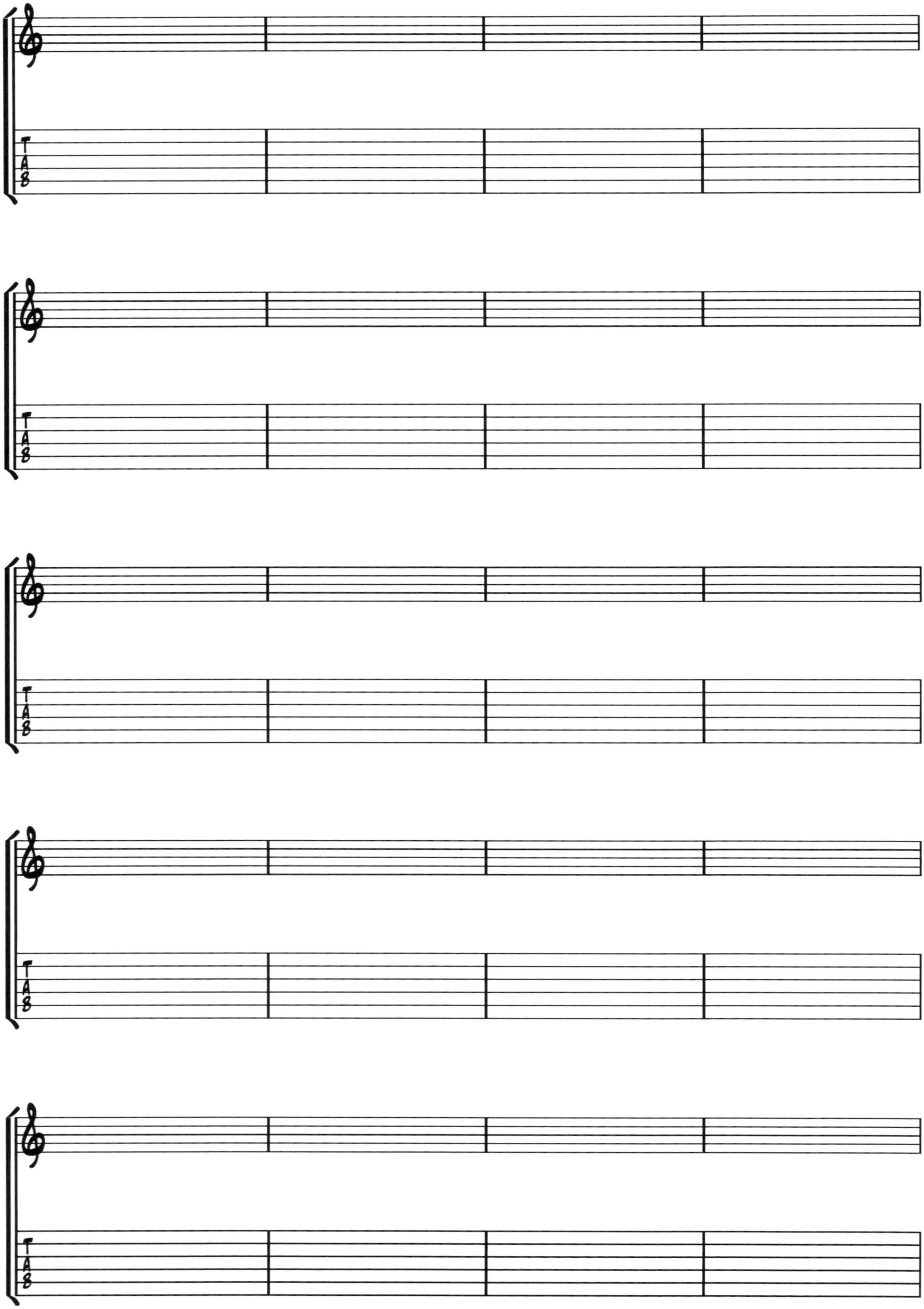

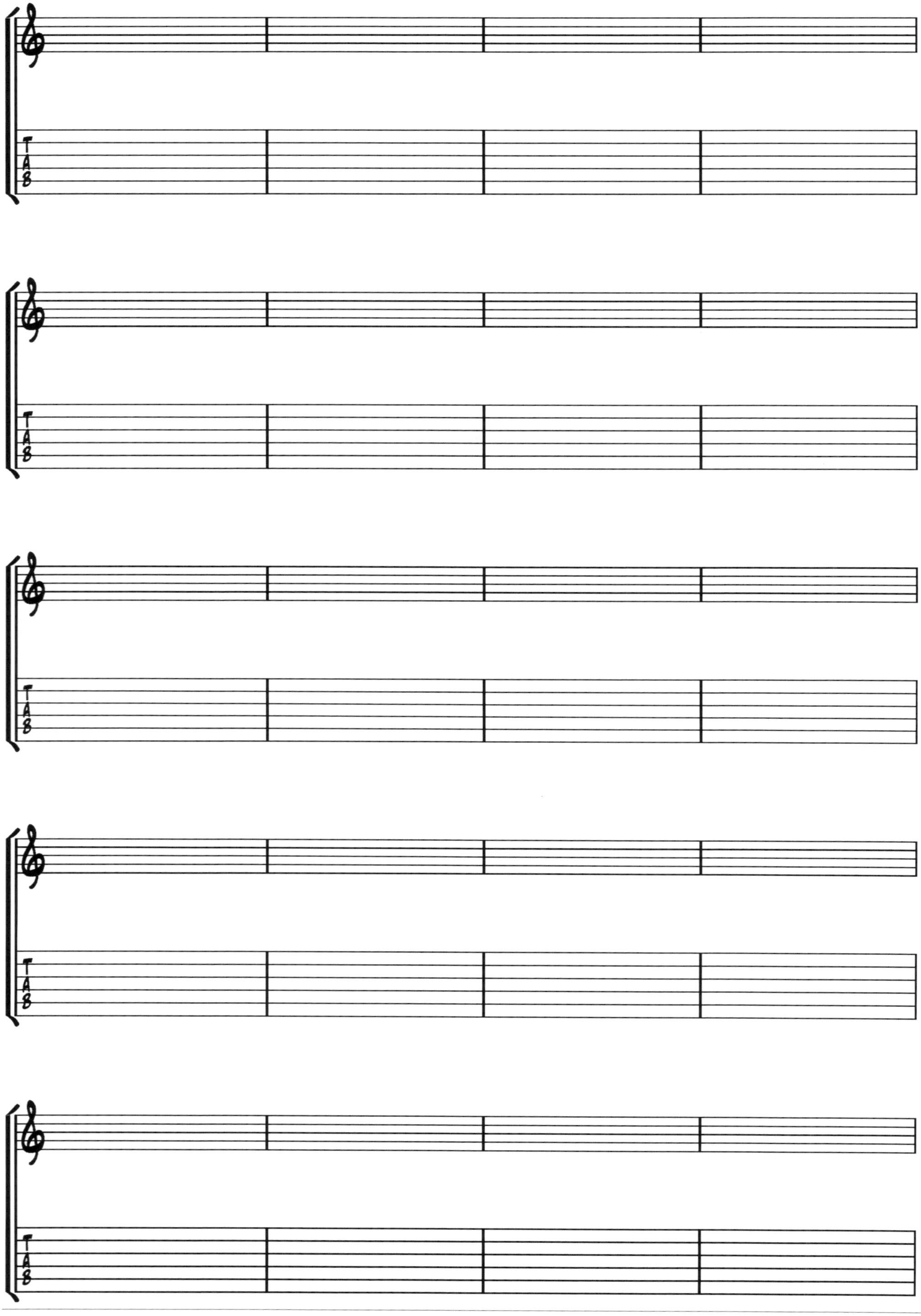

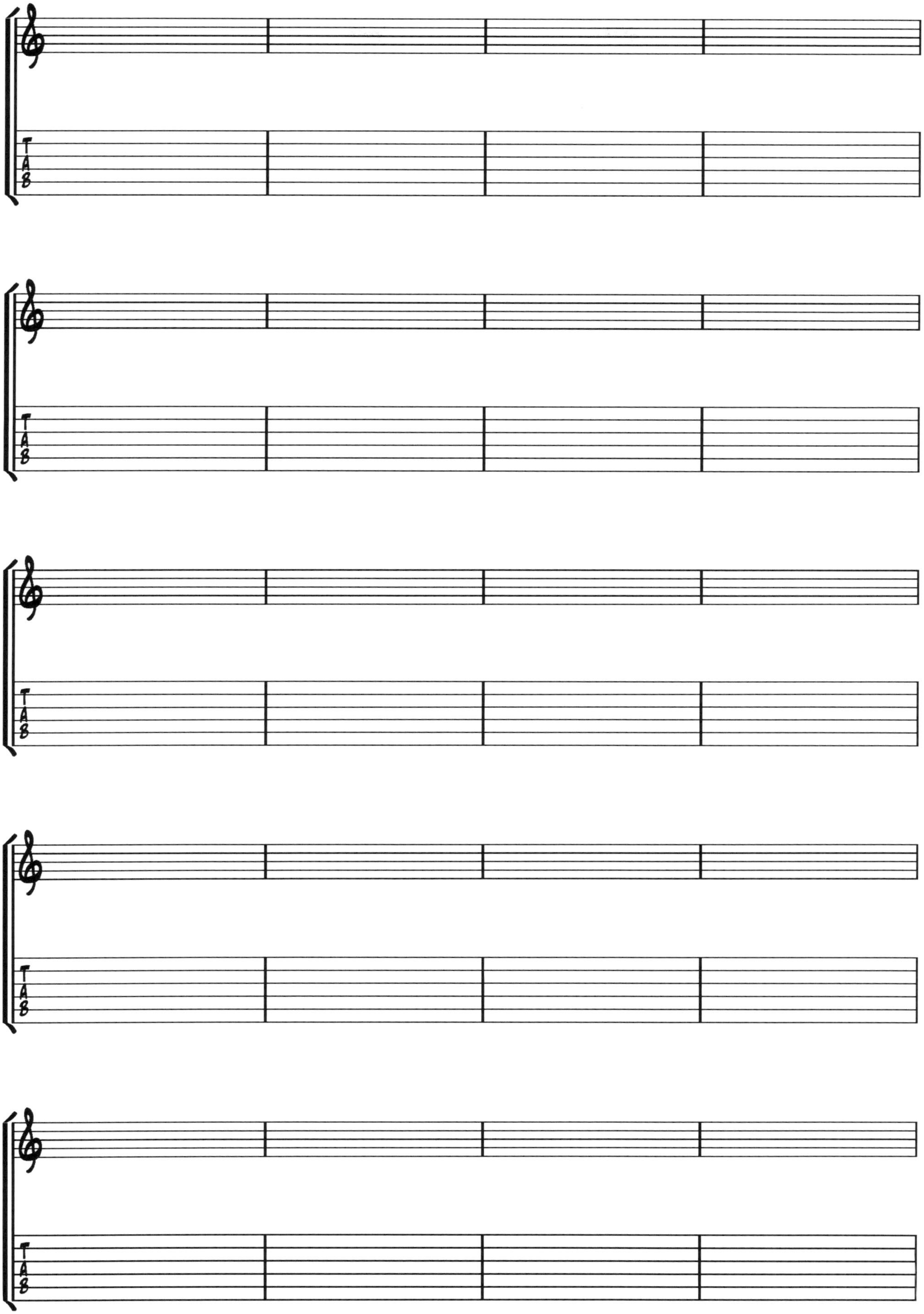

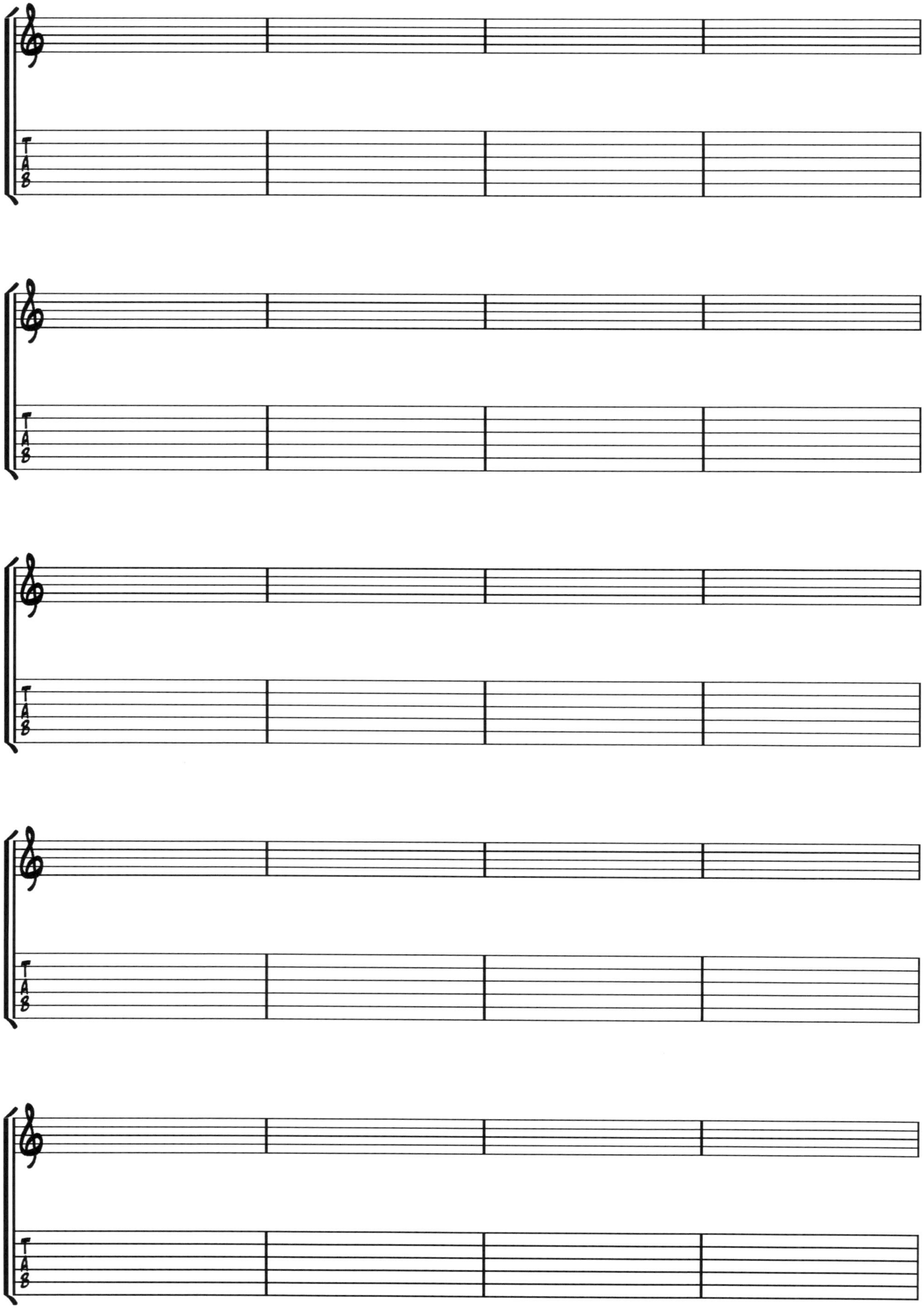

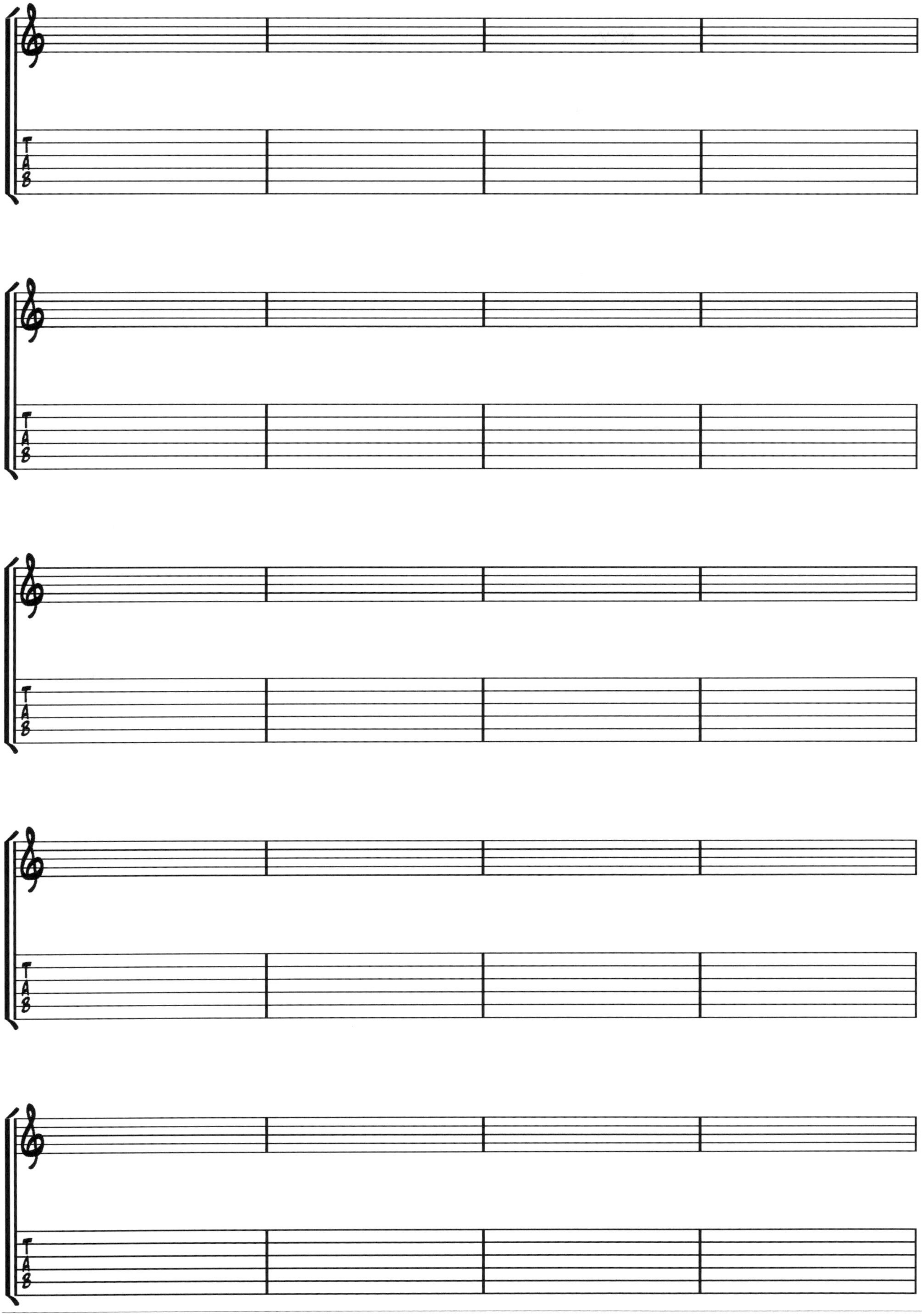

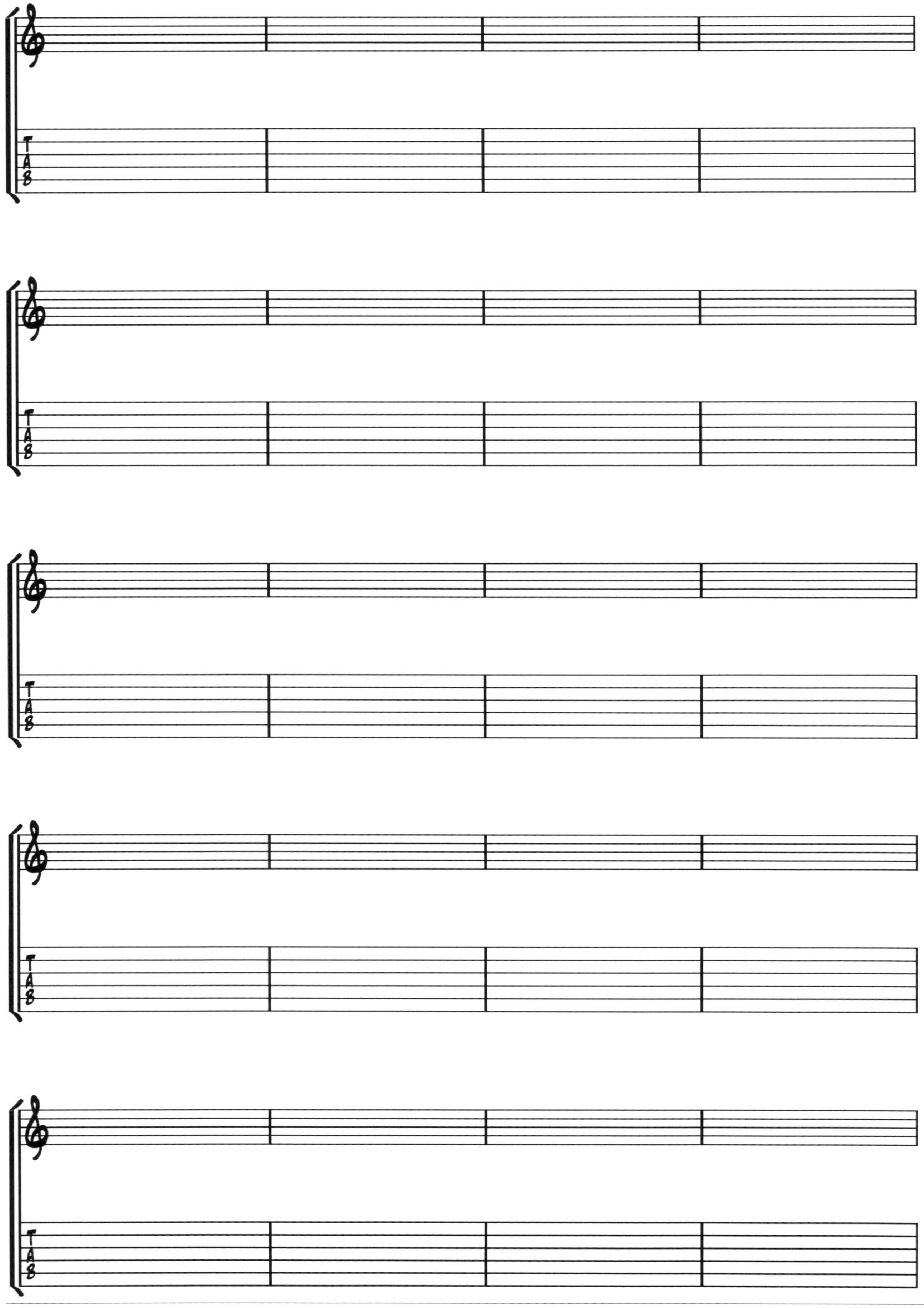

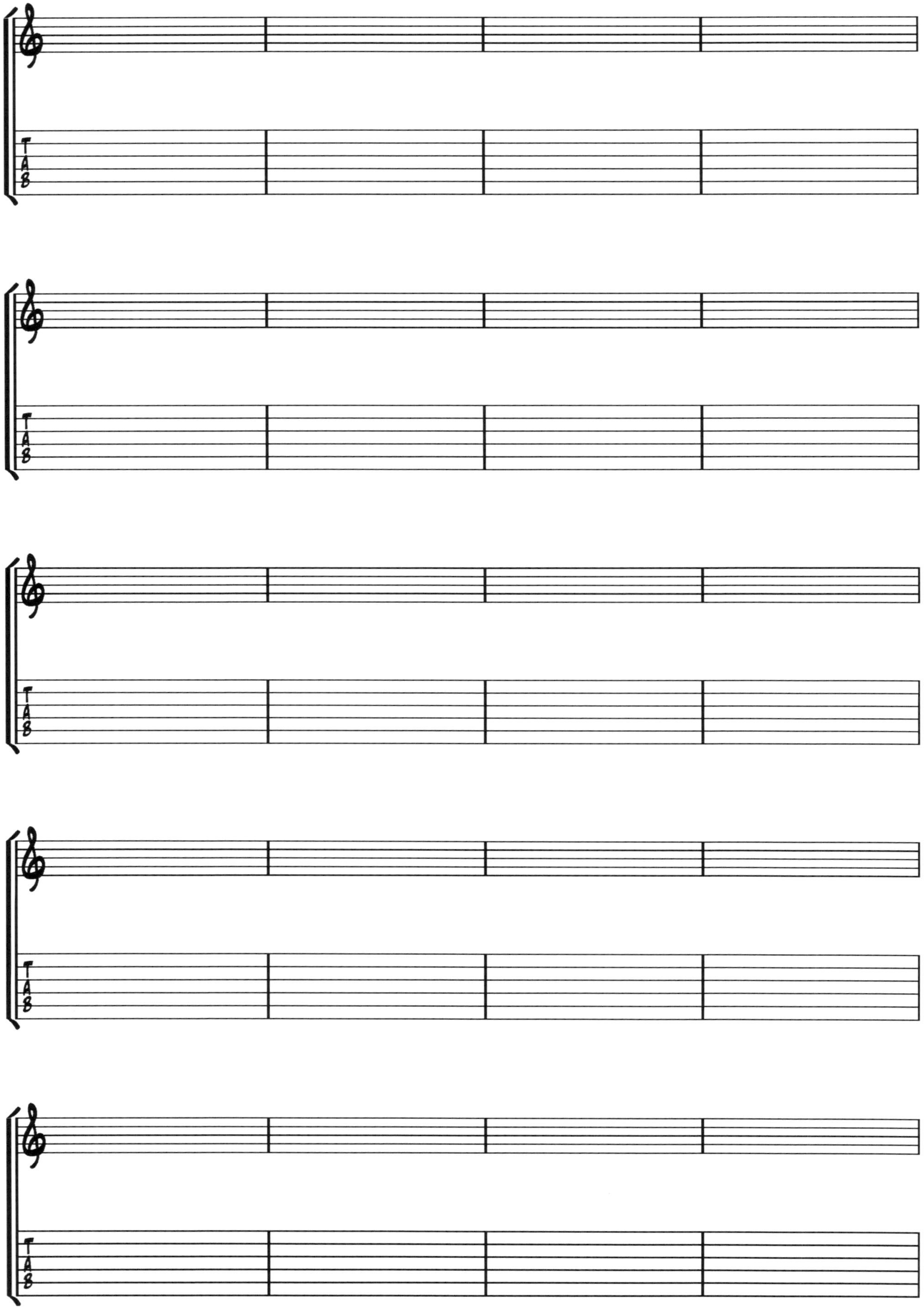

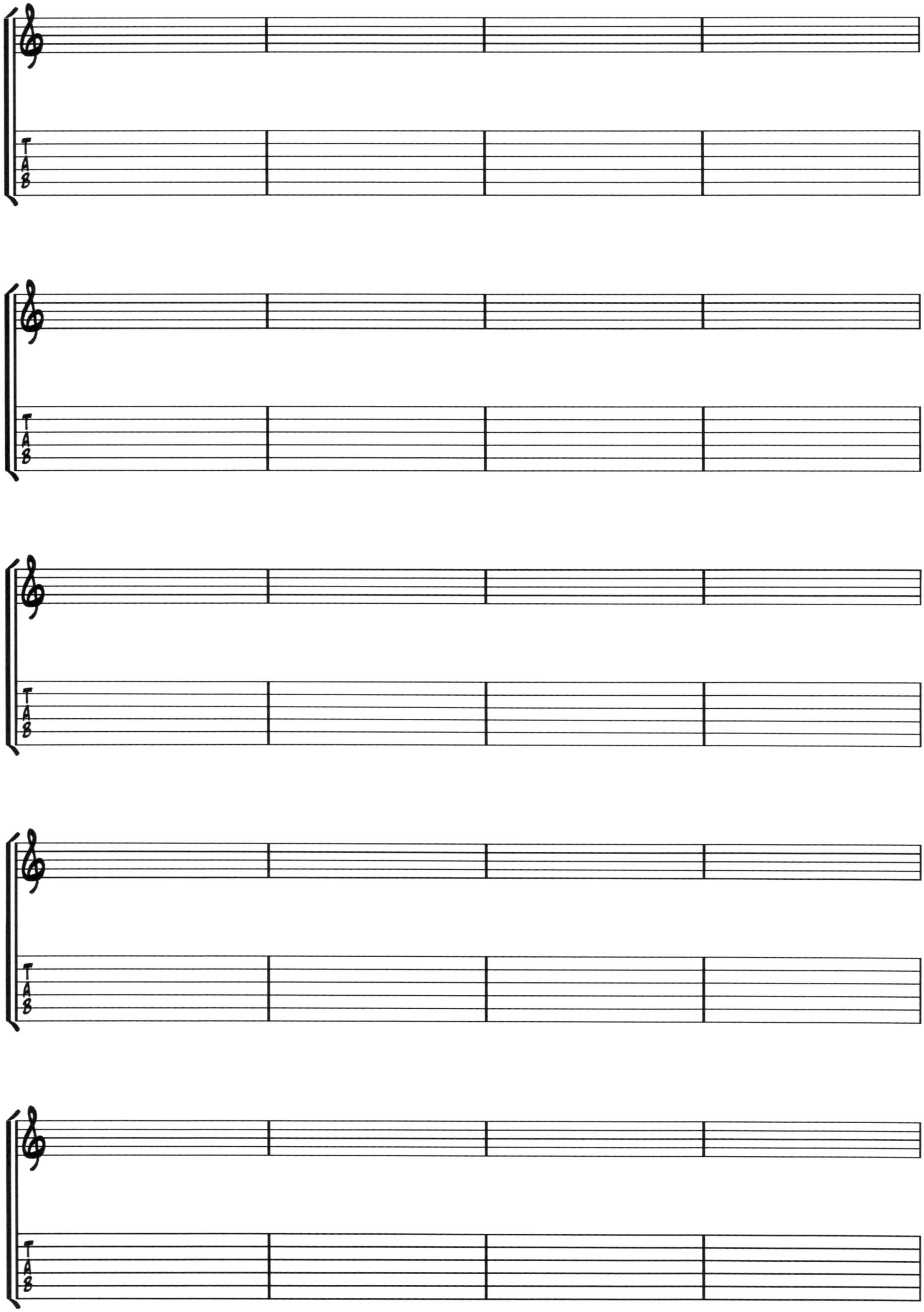

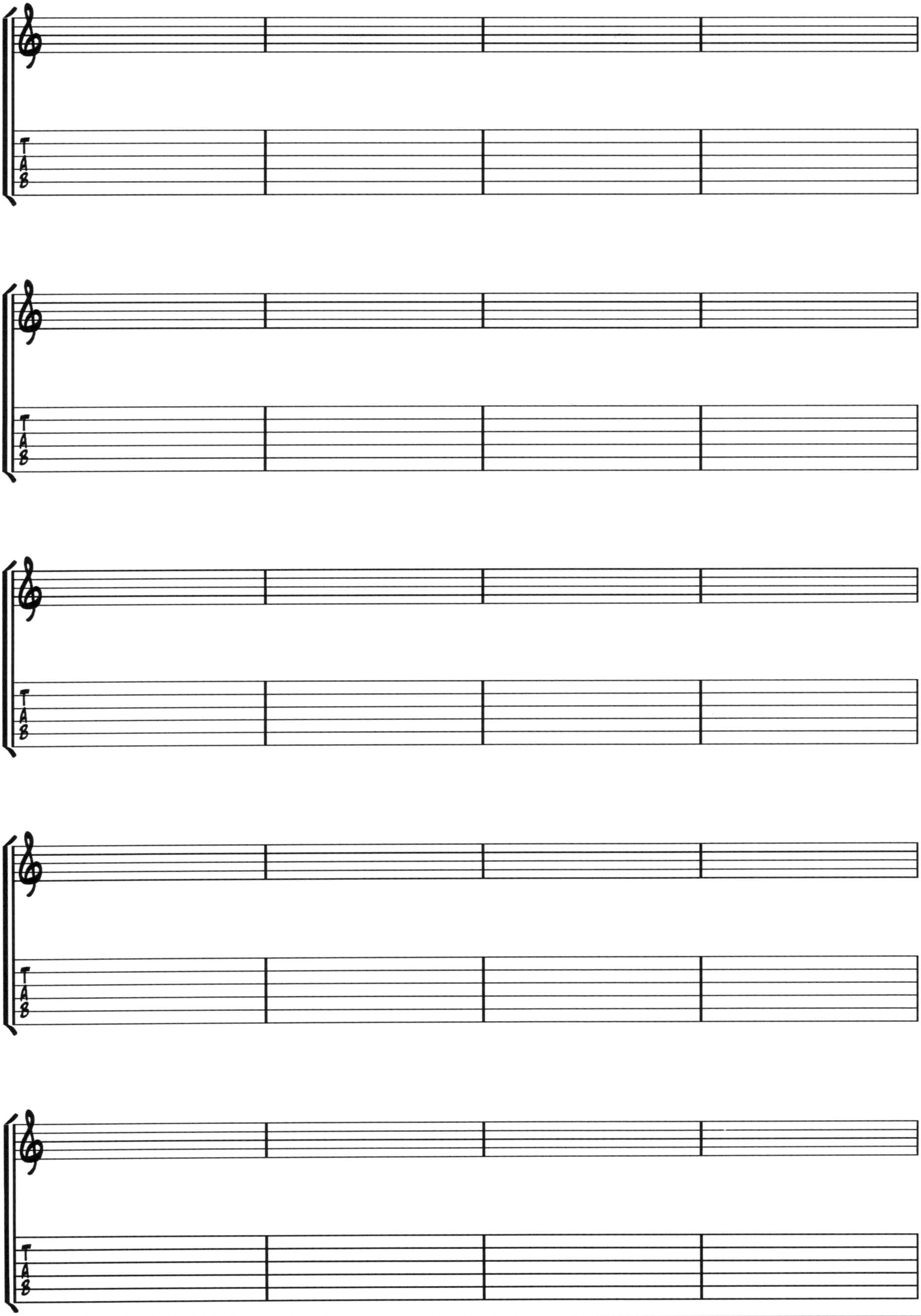

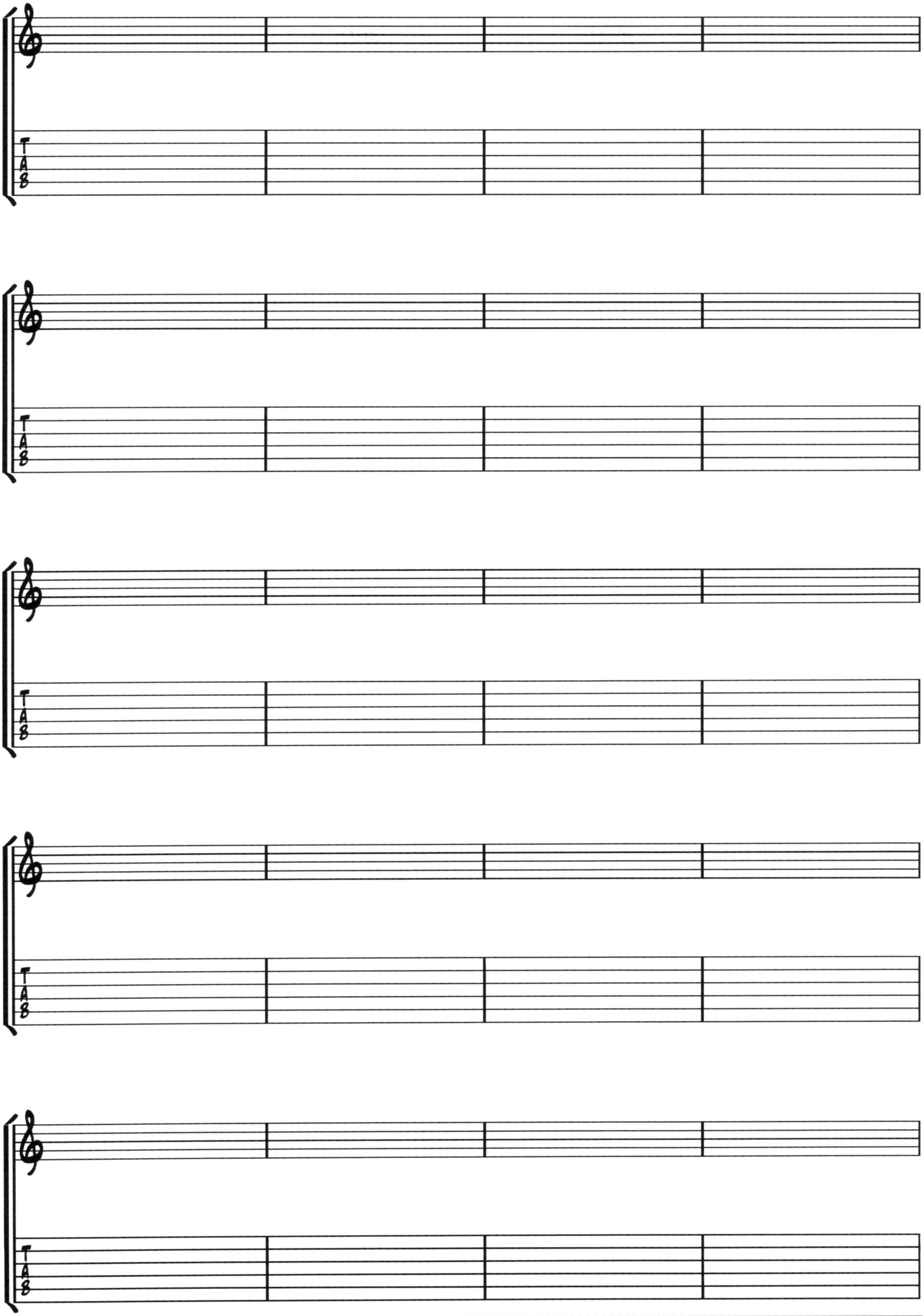

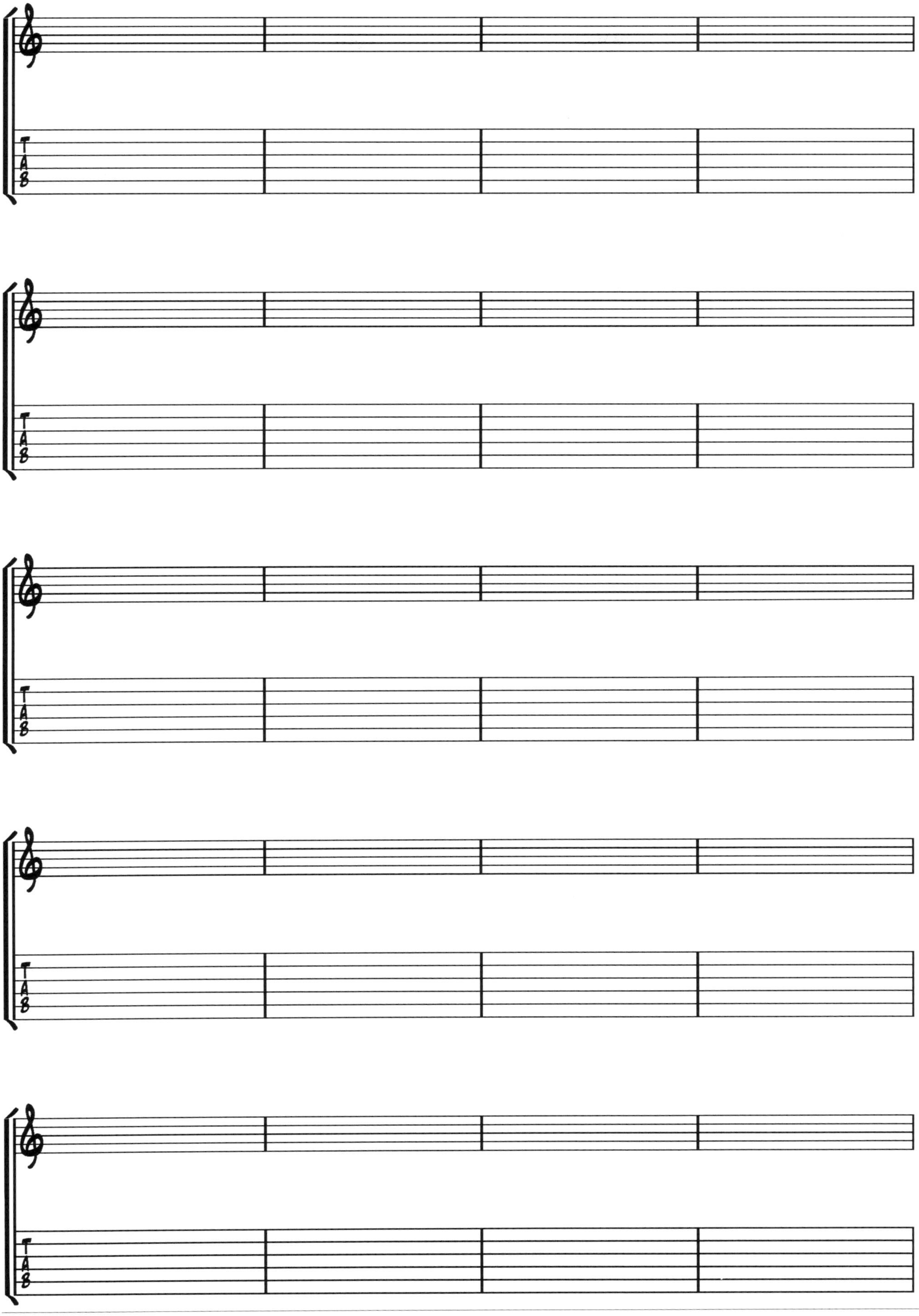

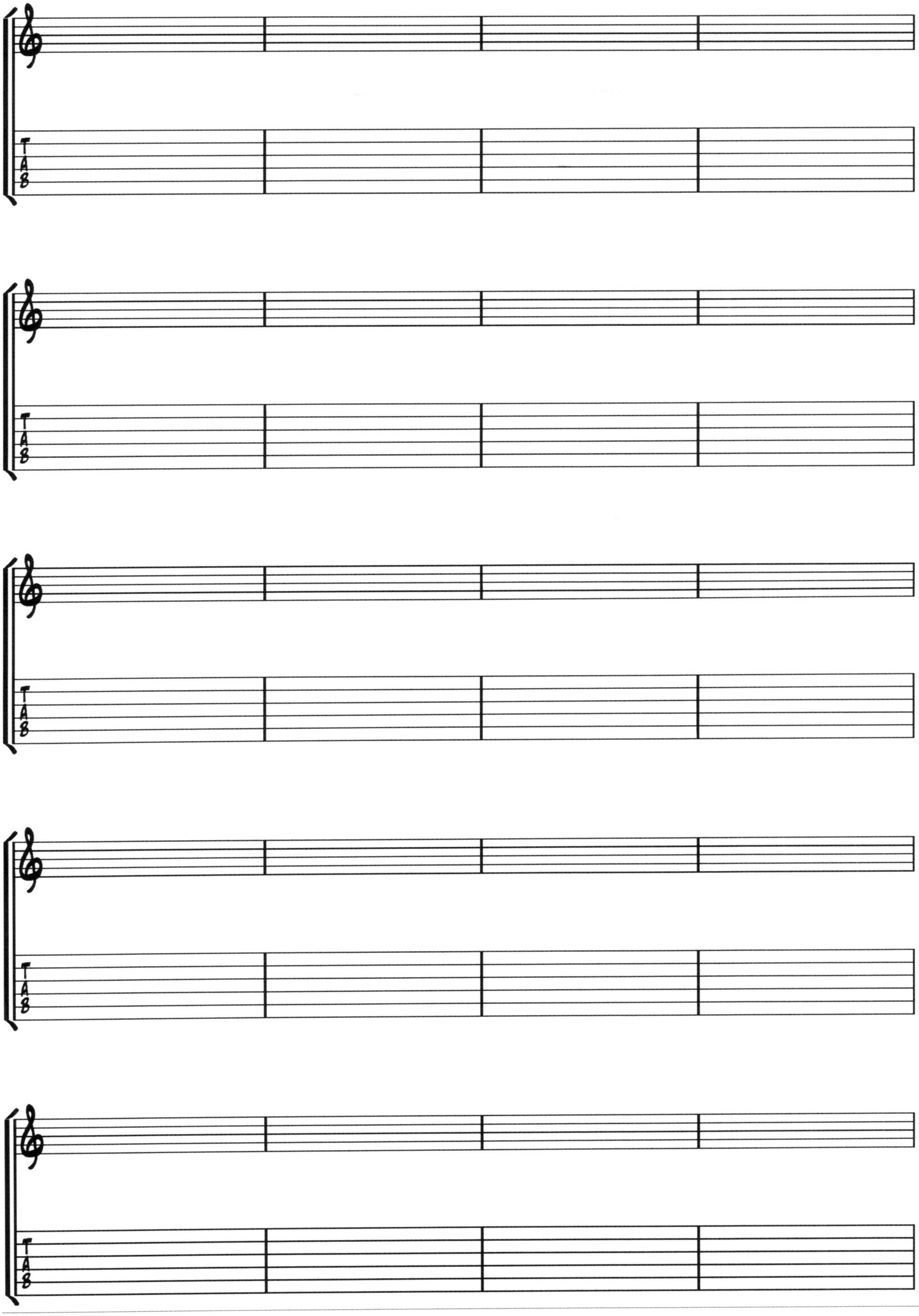

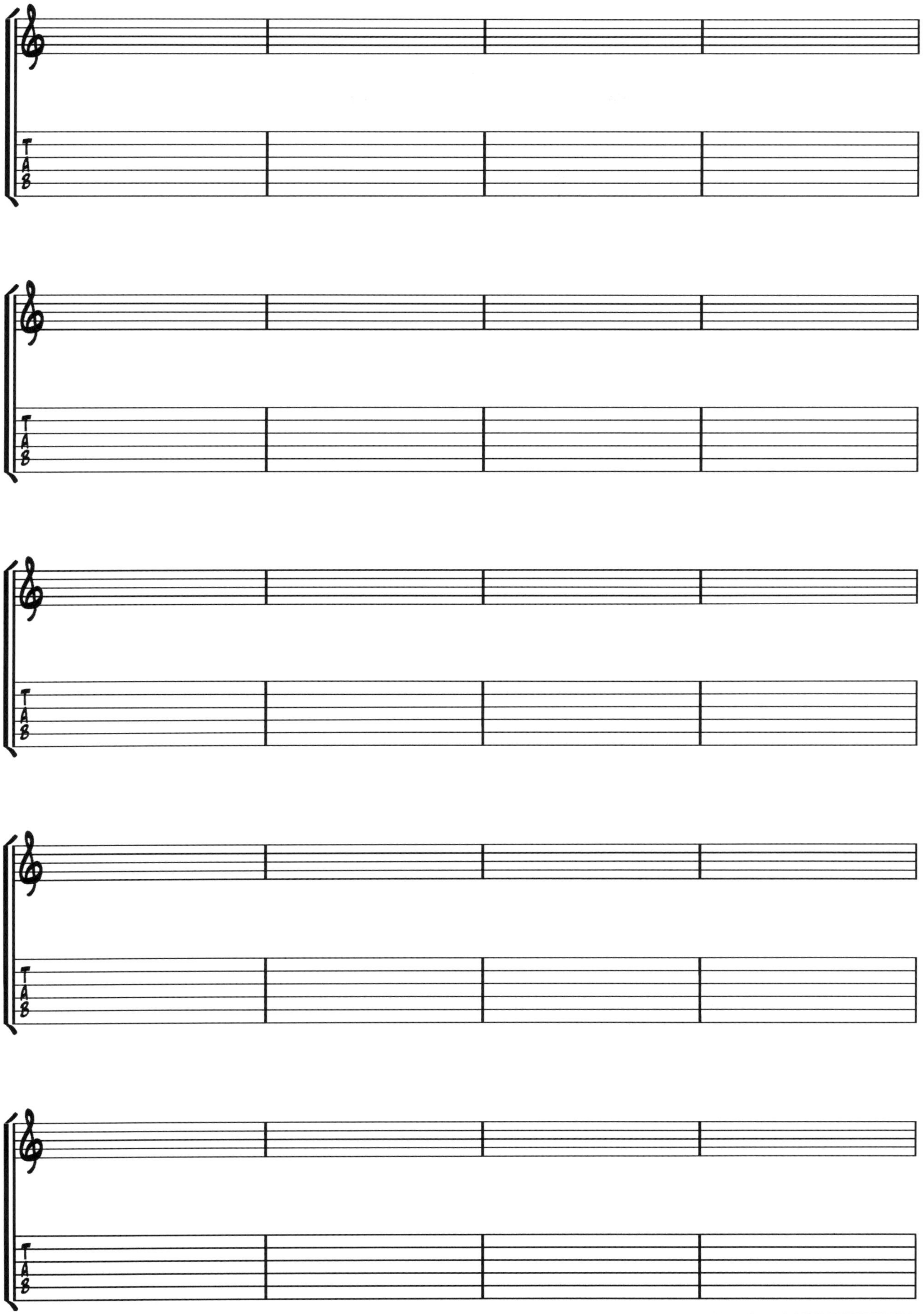

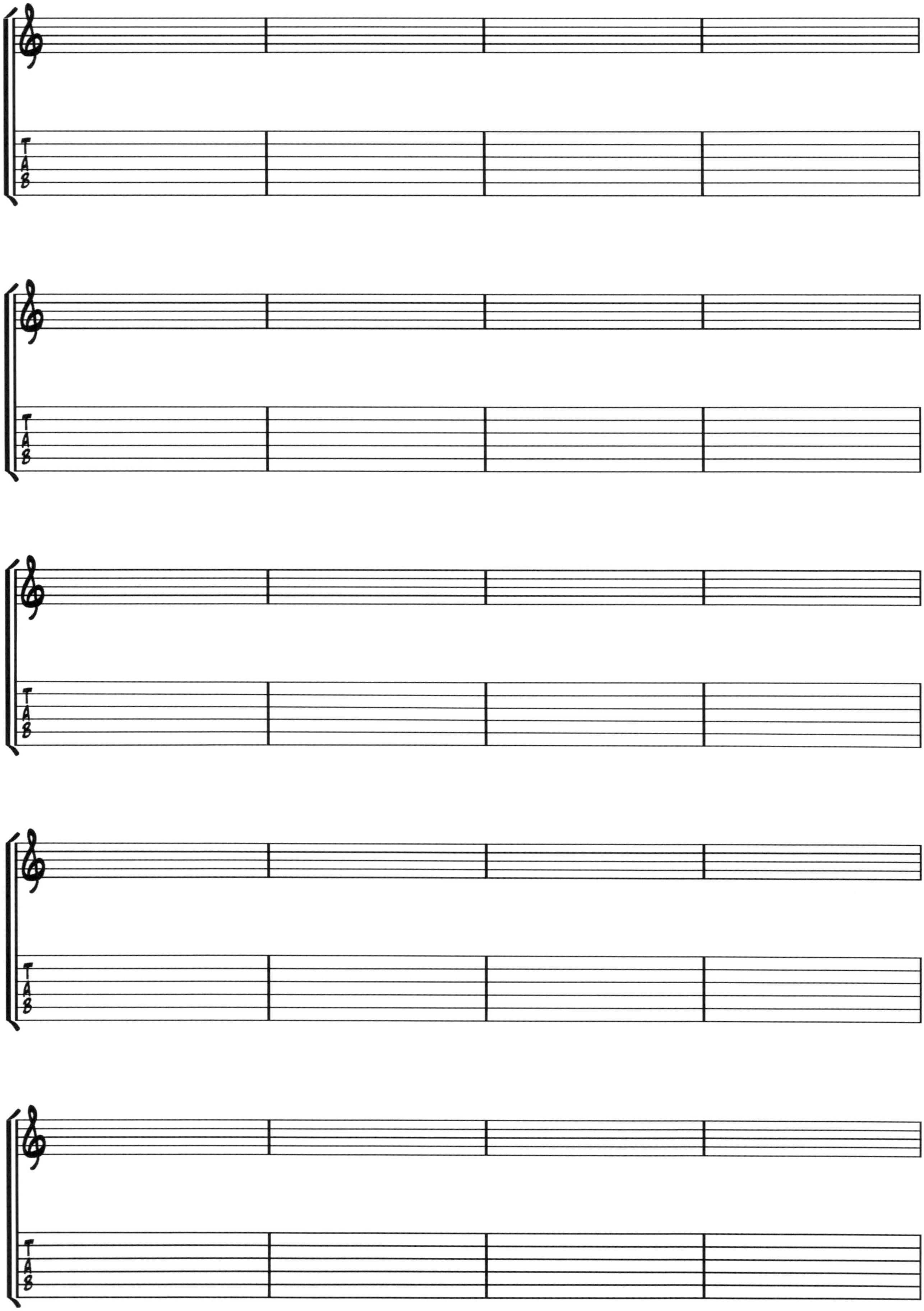

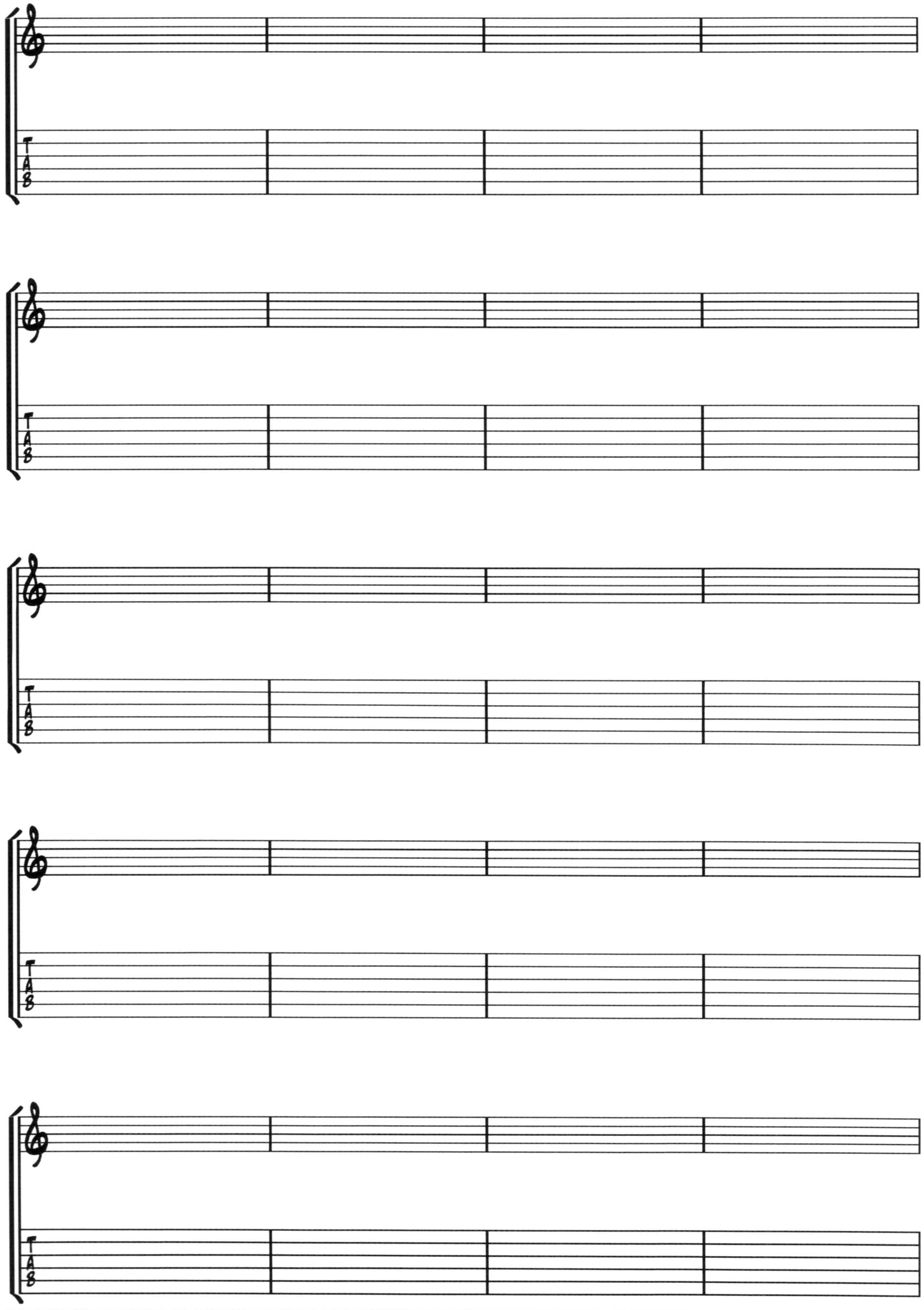

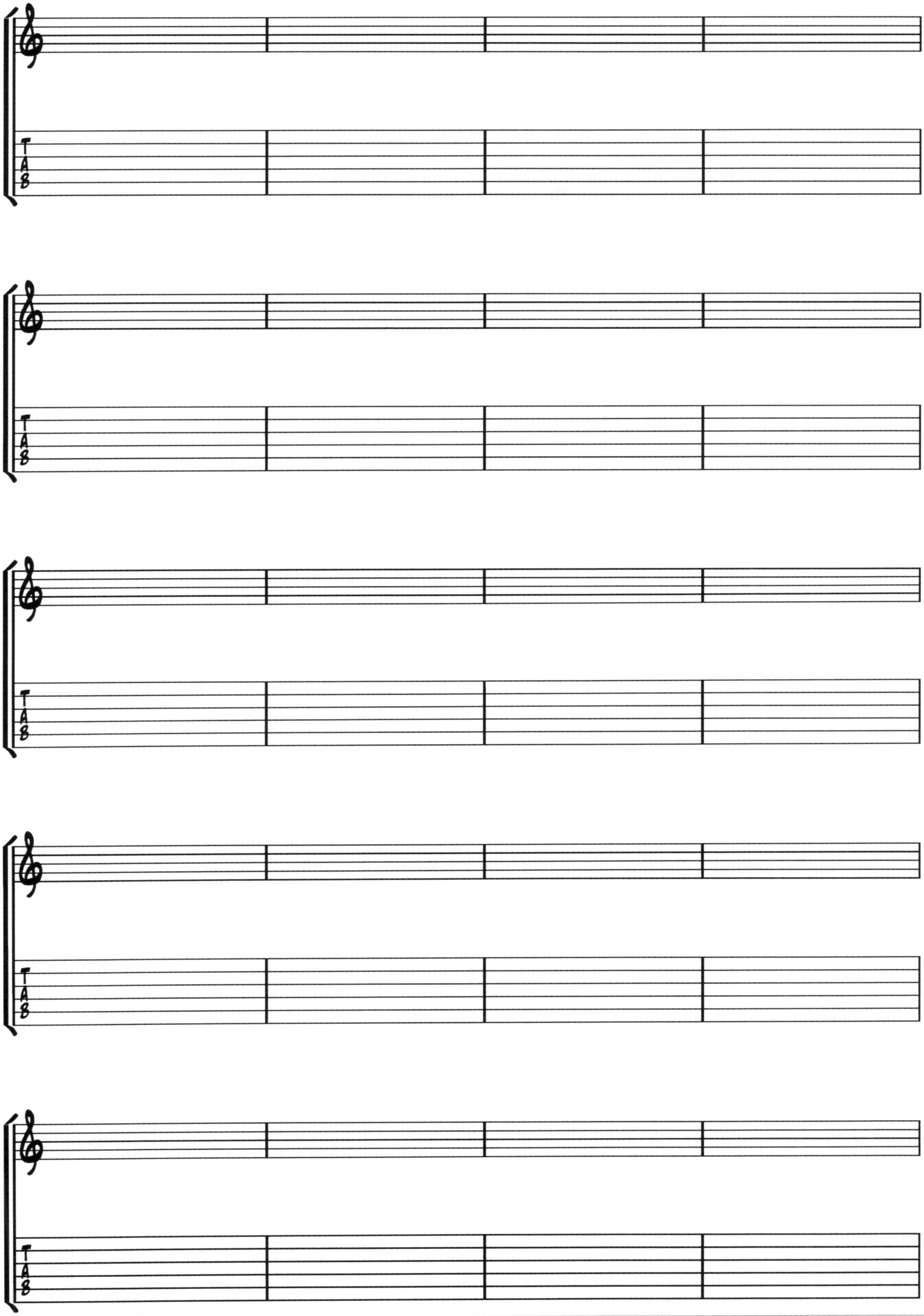

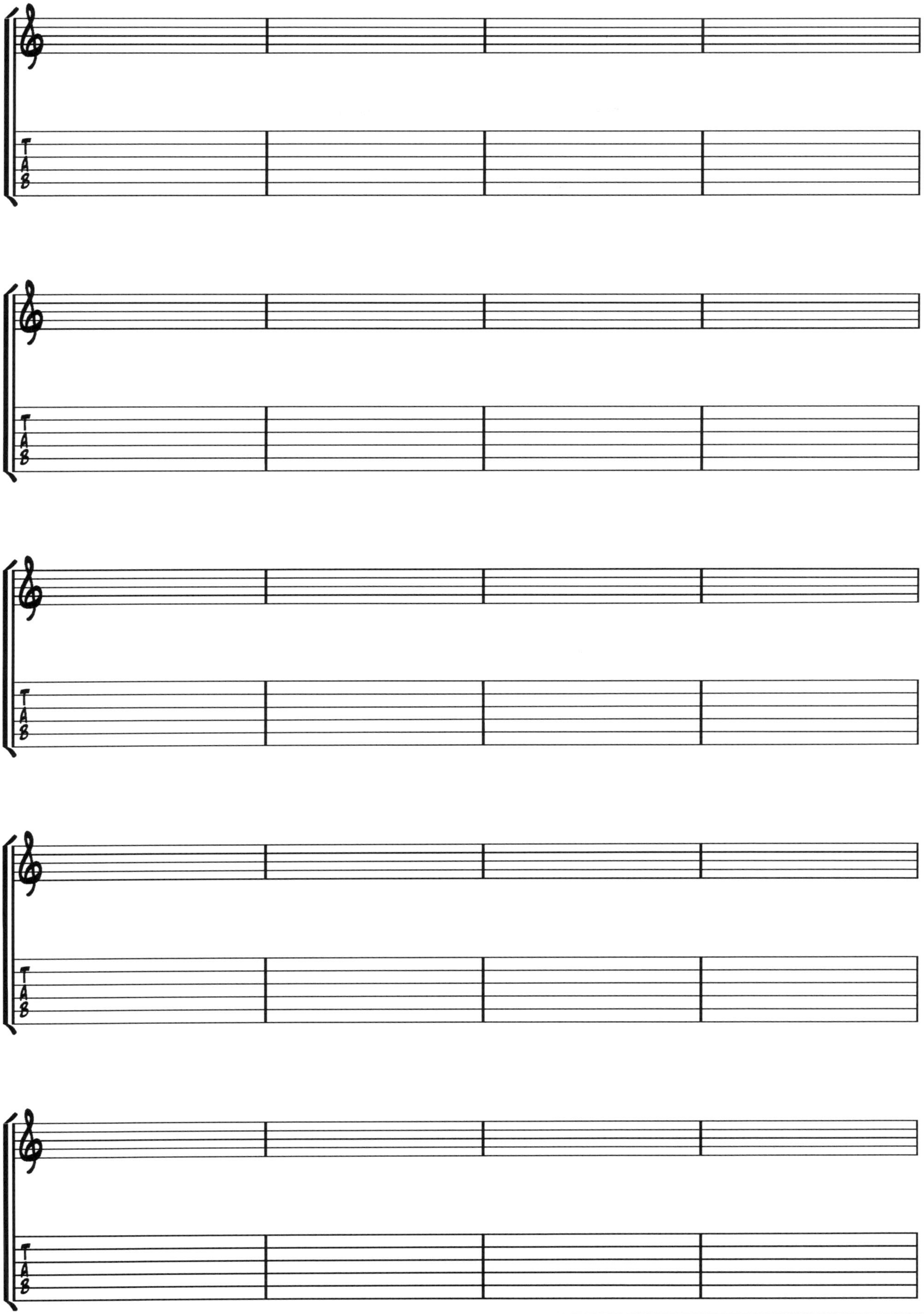
TAB
TAB
TAB
TAB
TAB

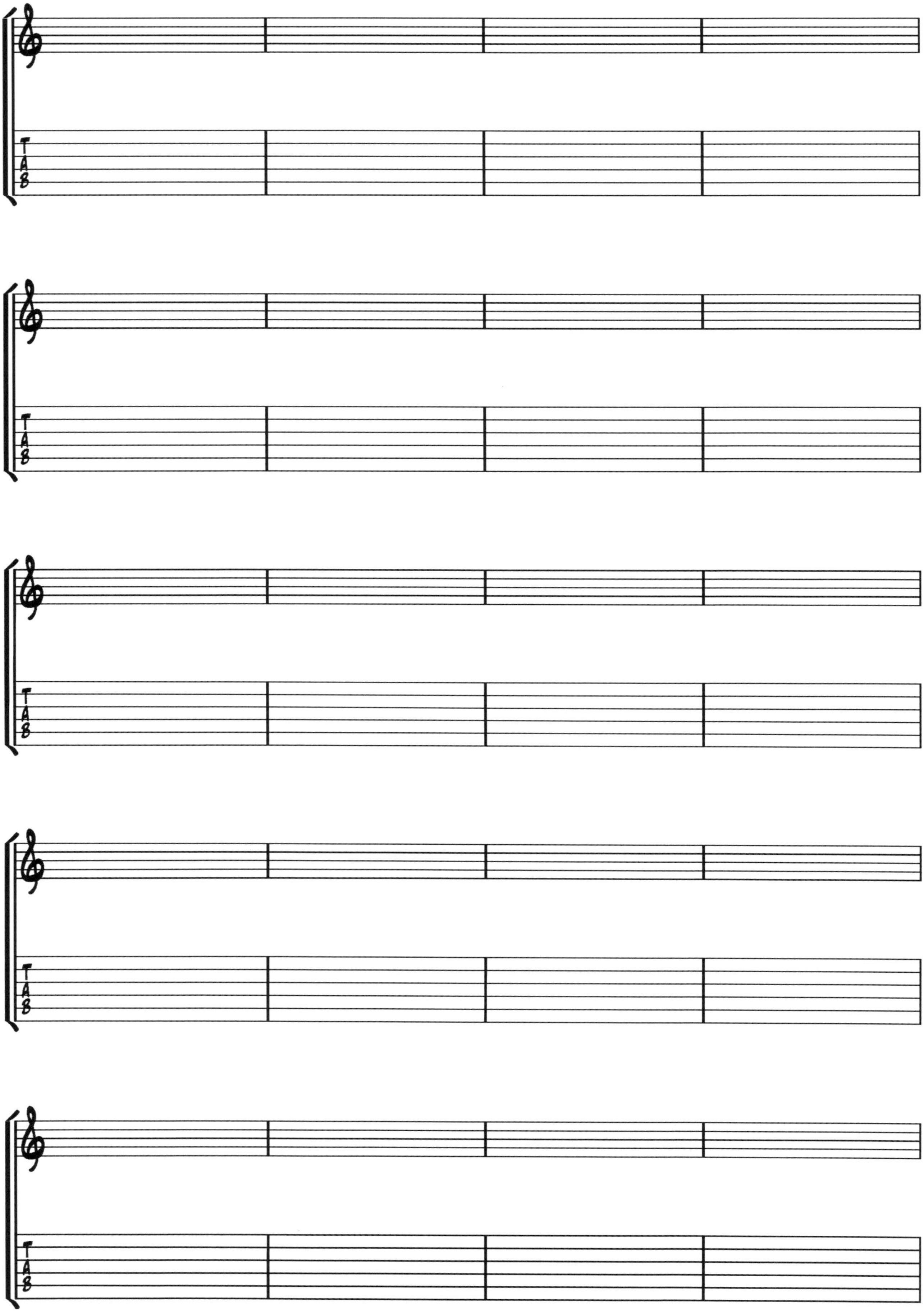

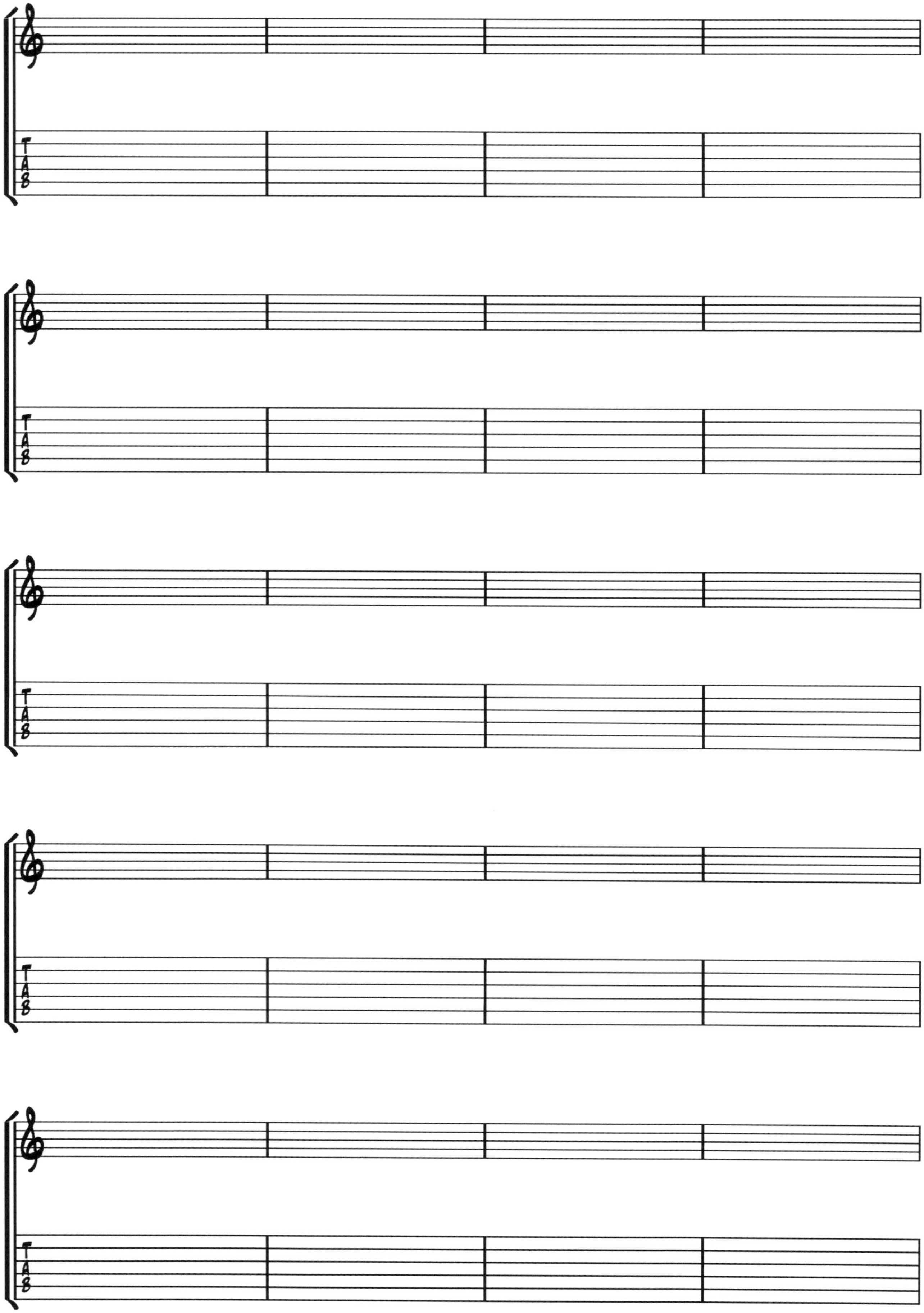

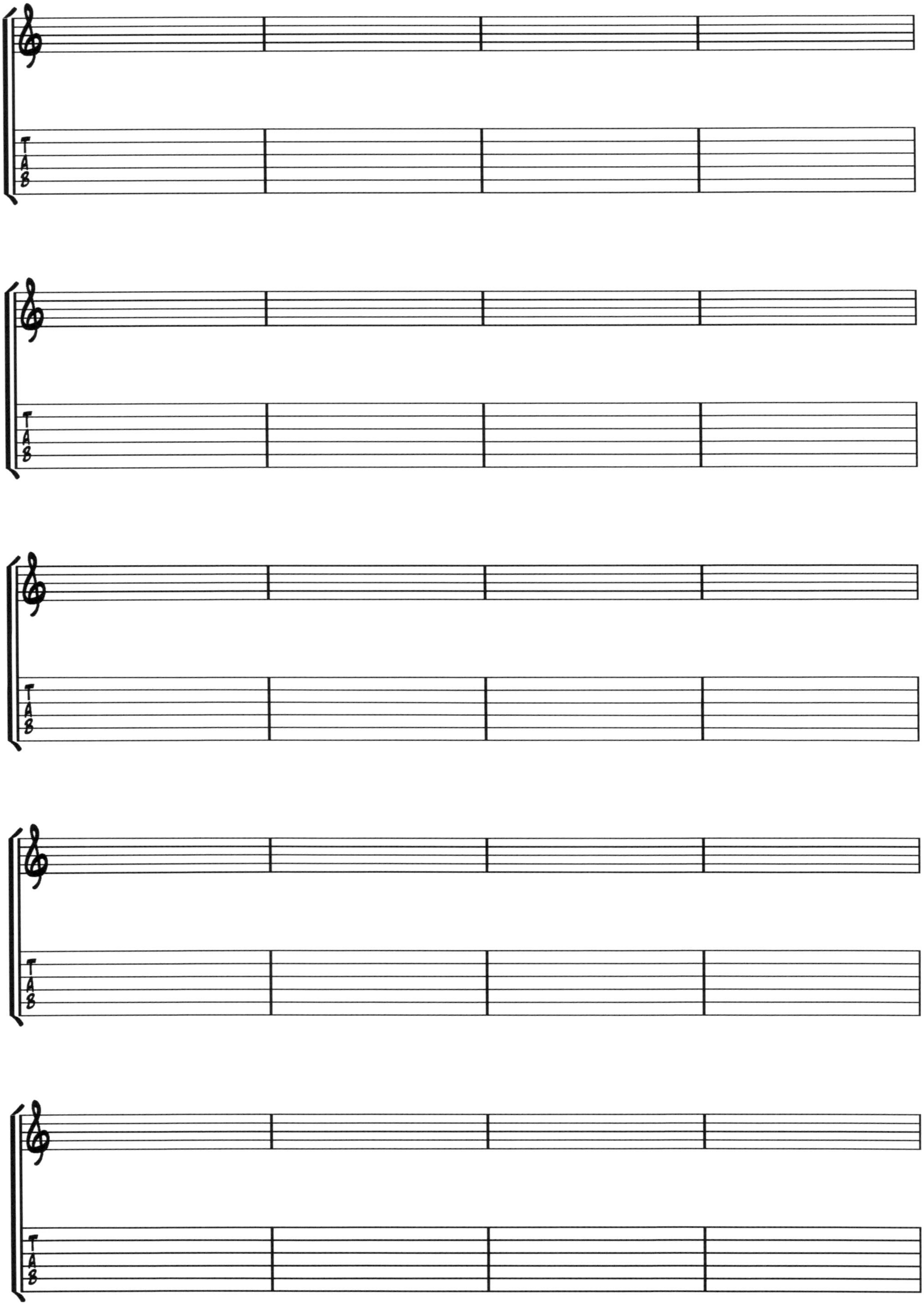

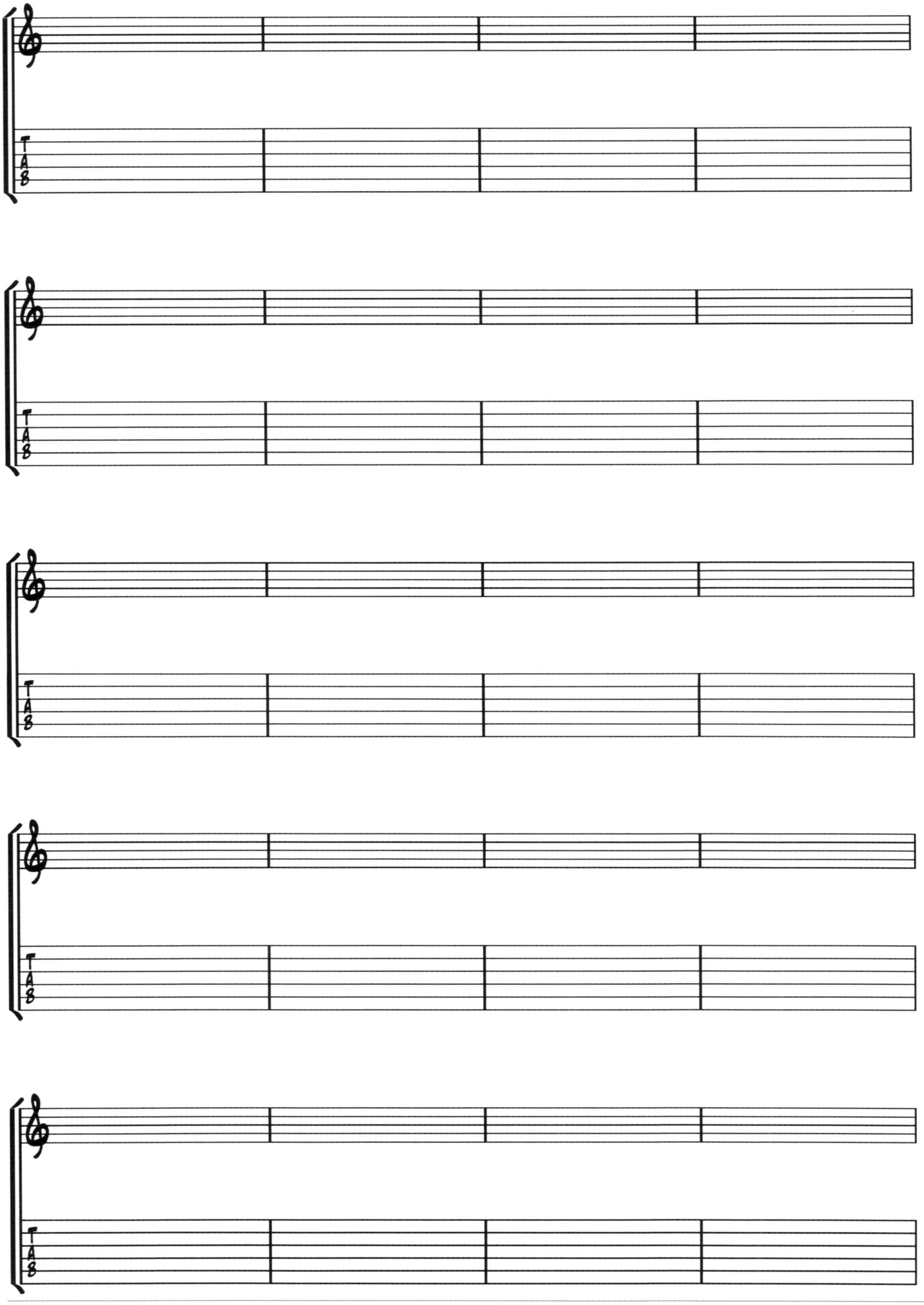

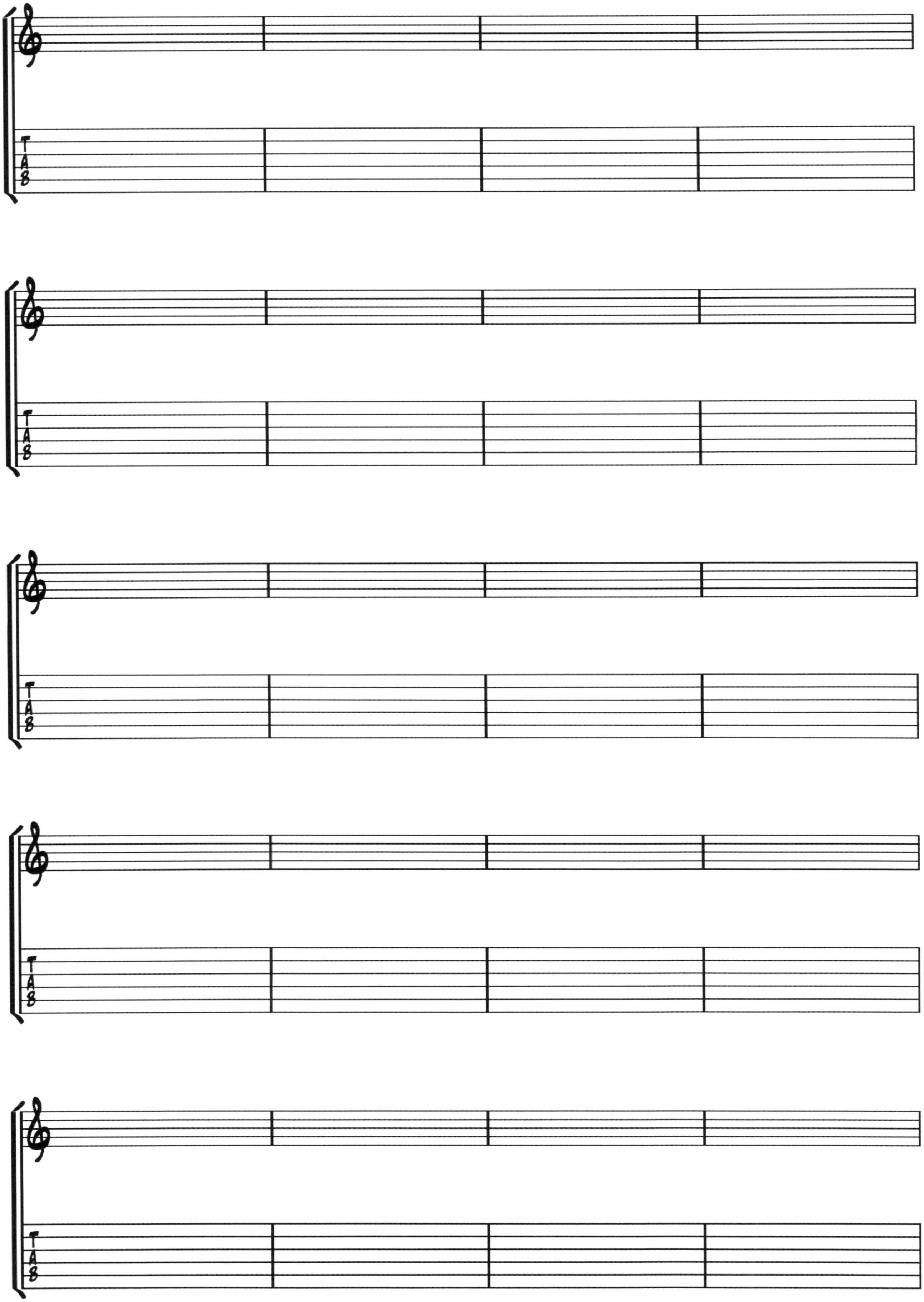

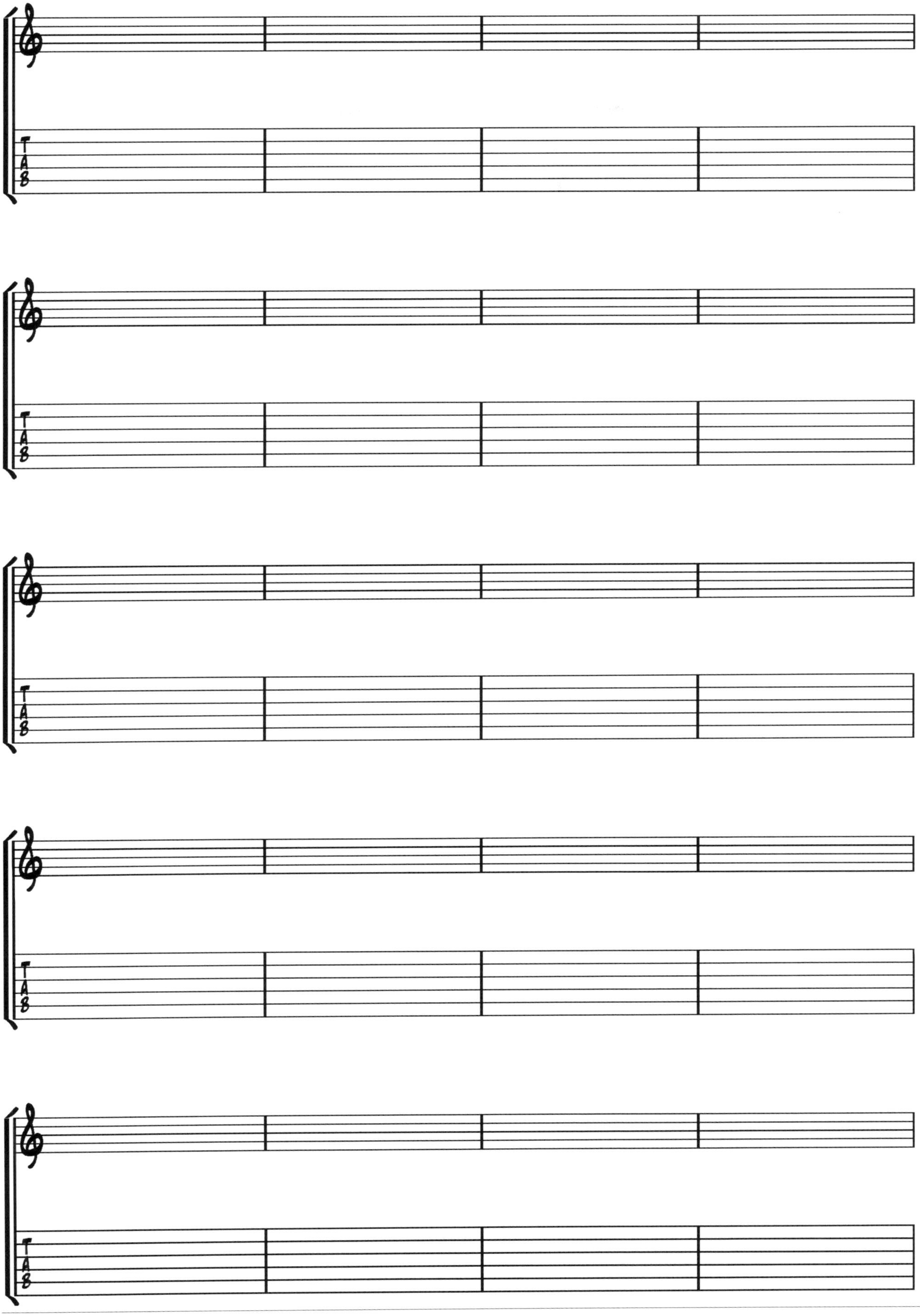

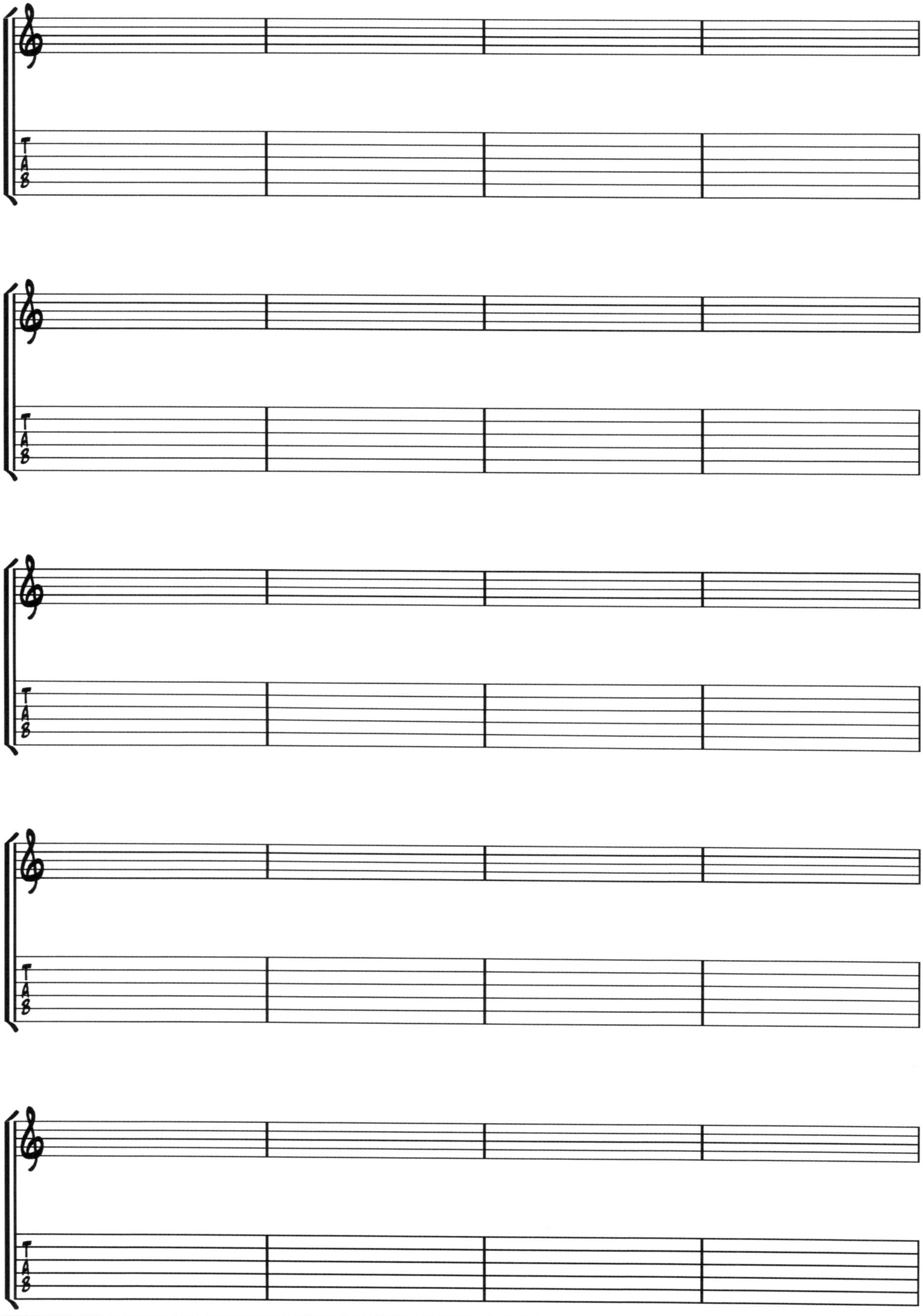

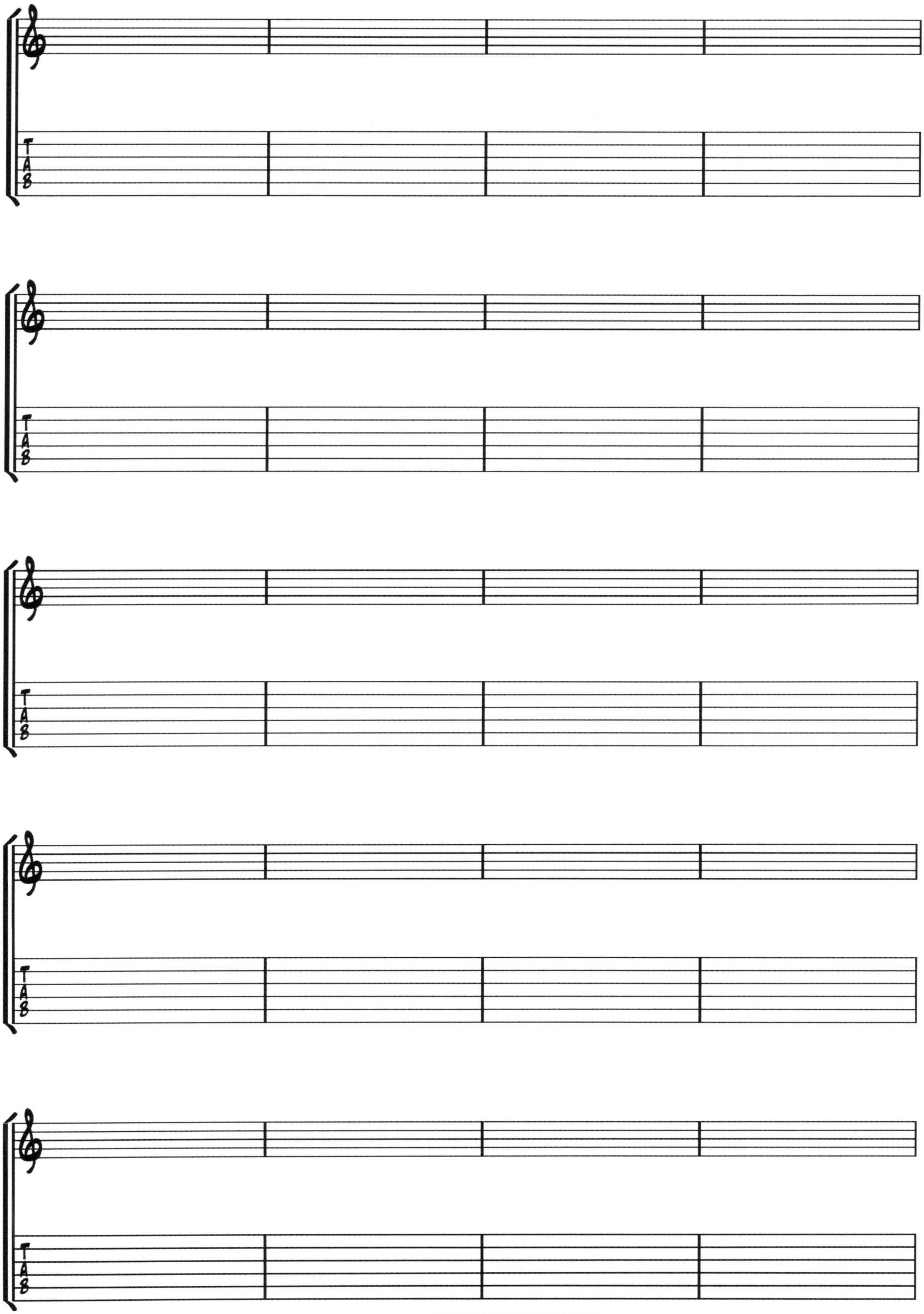

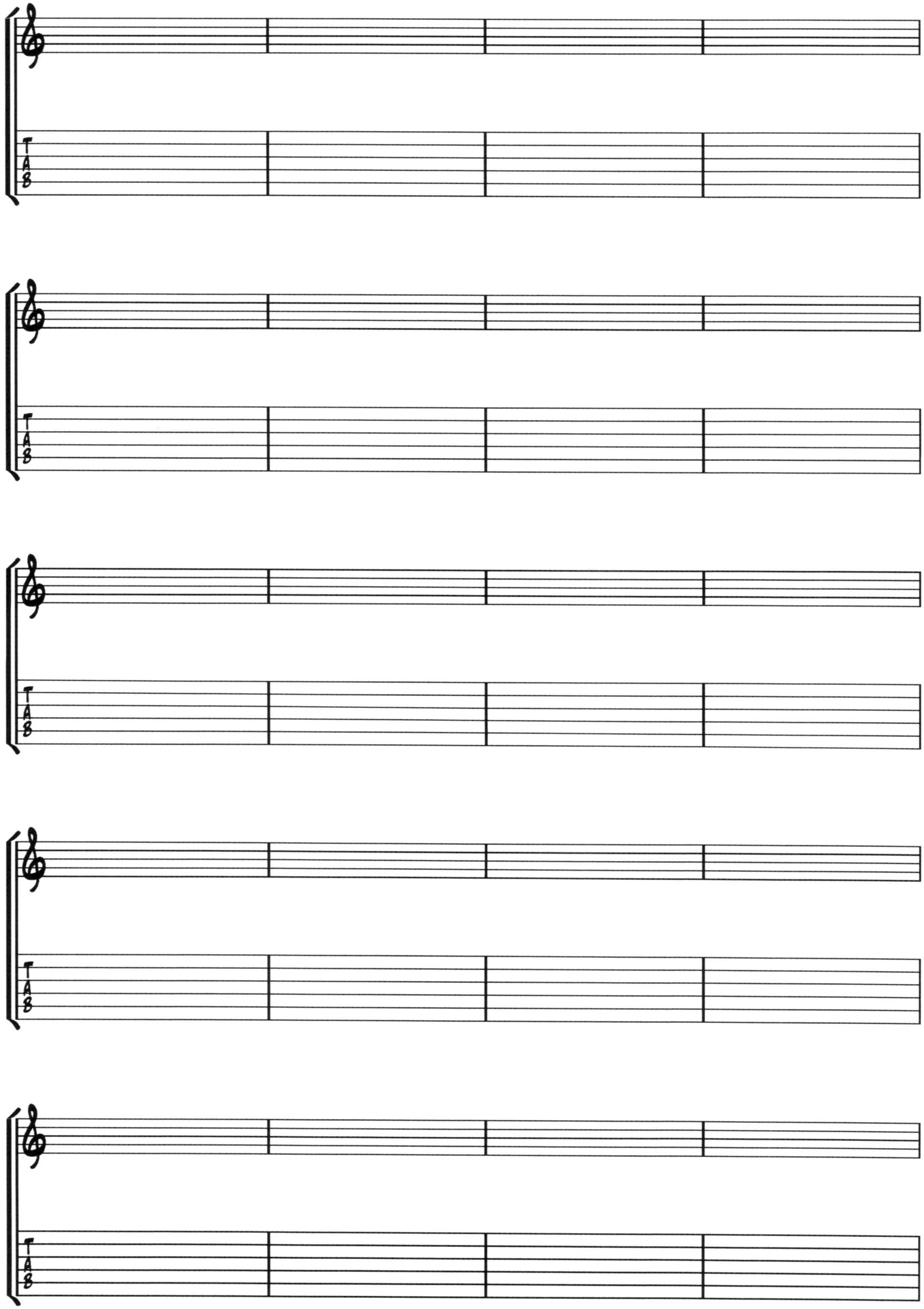

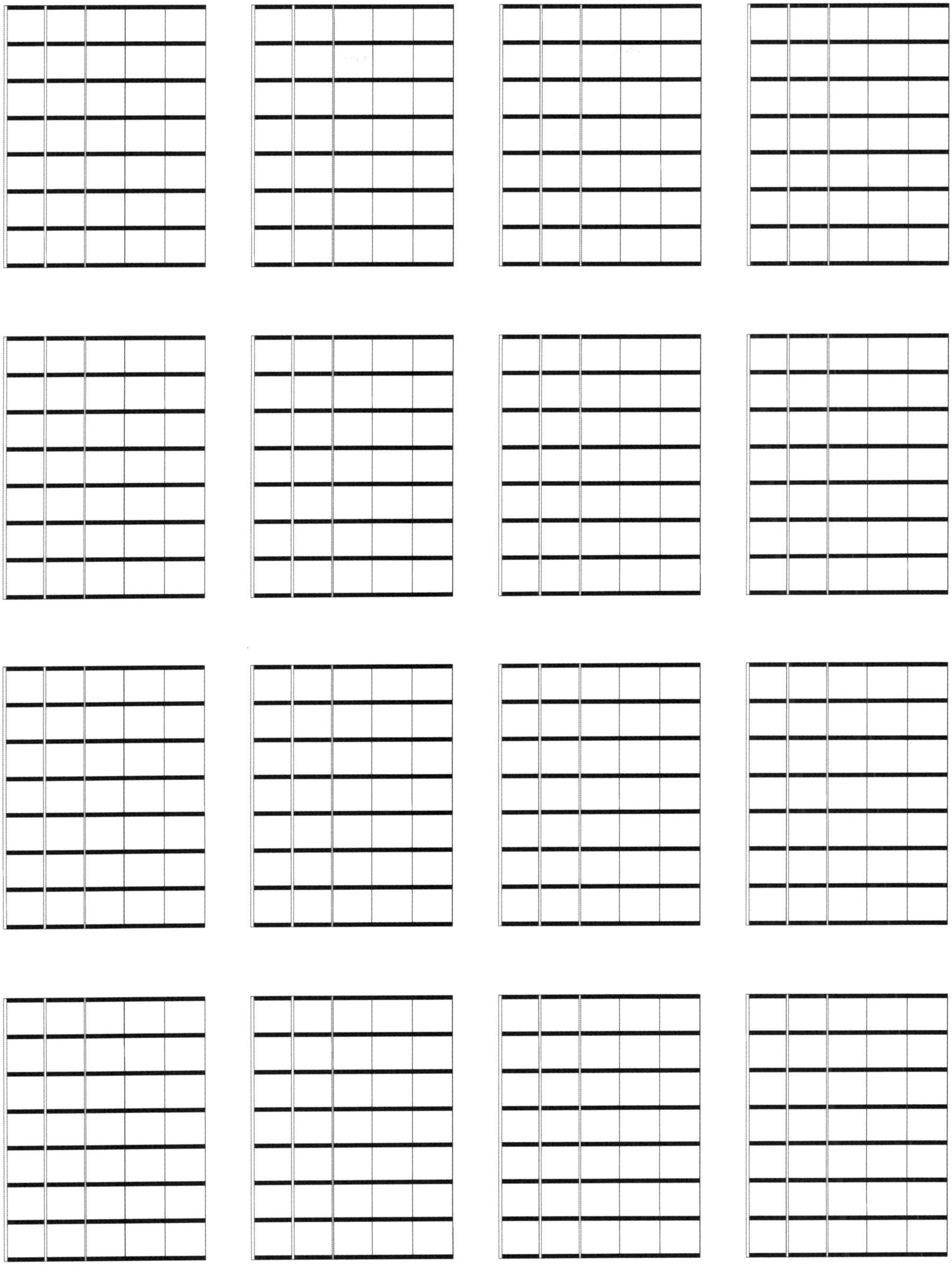

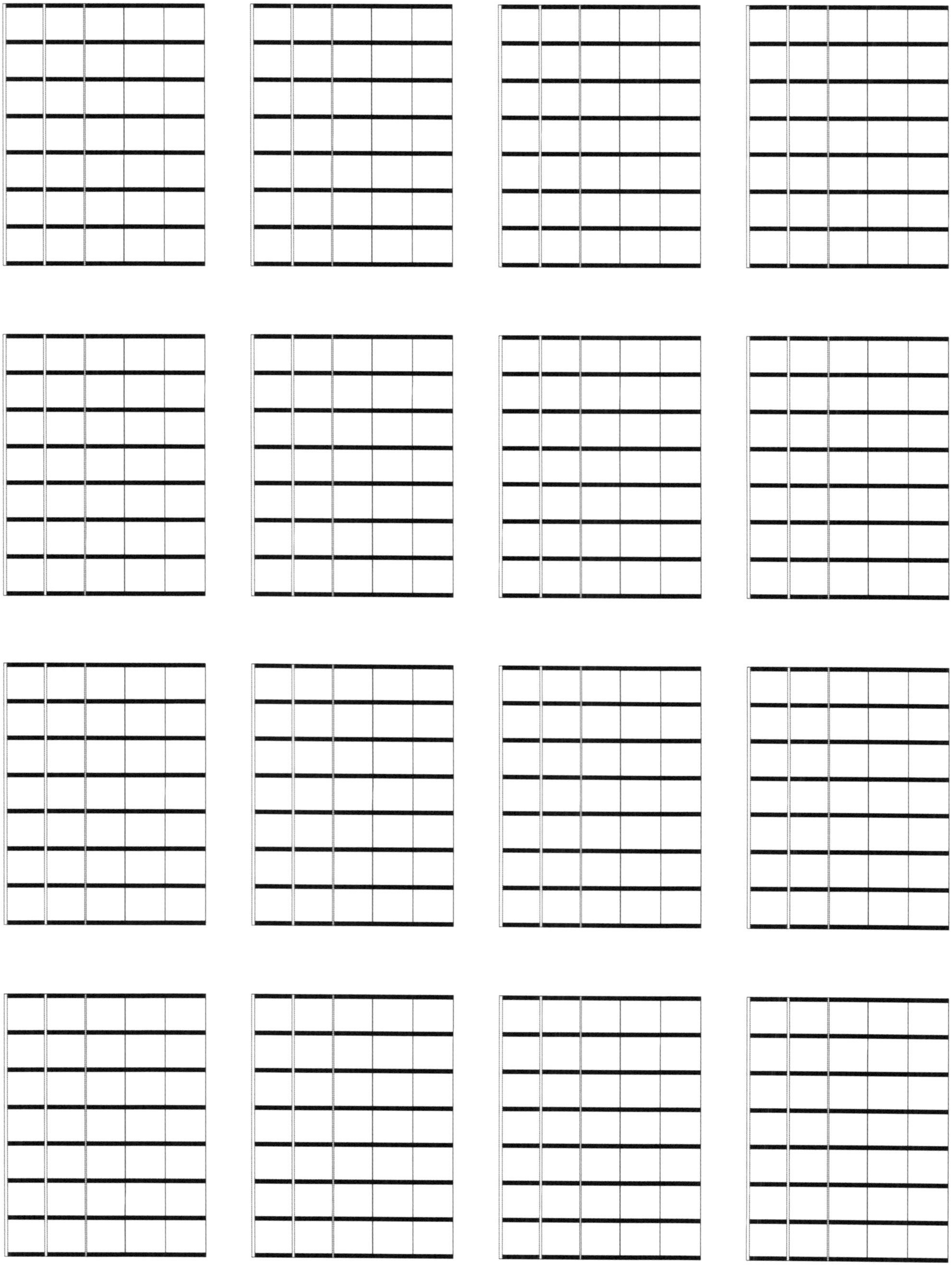

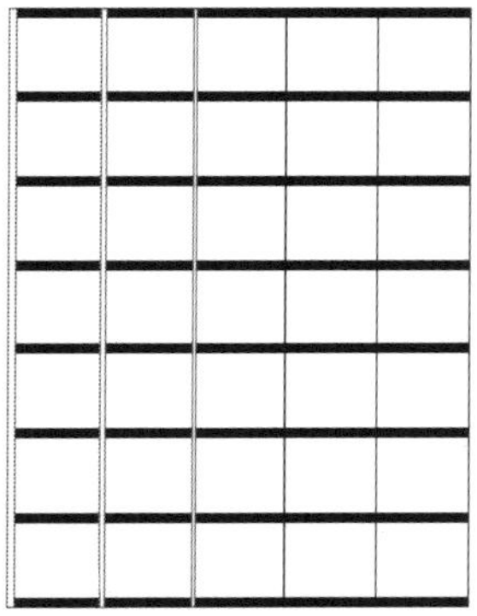
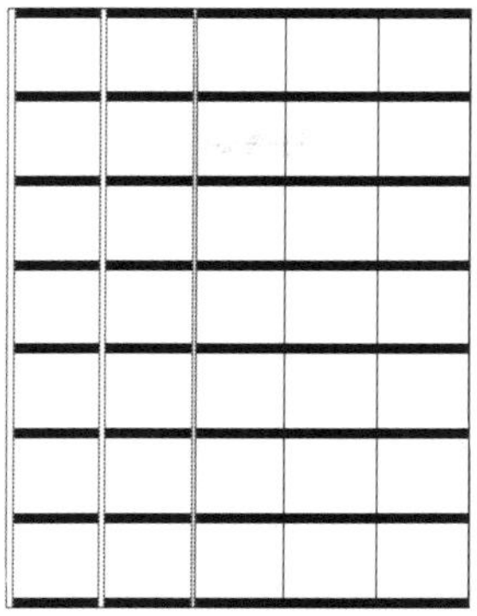
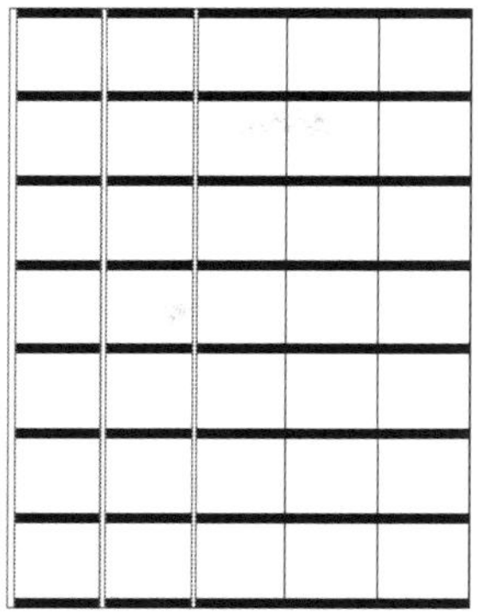
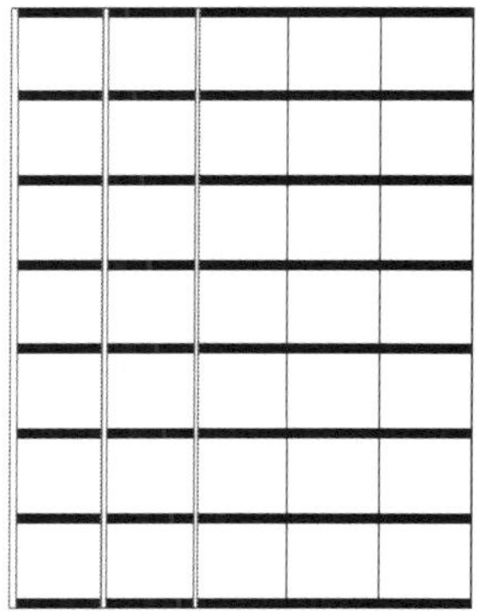
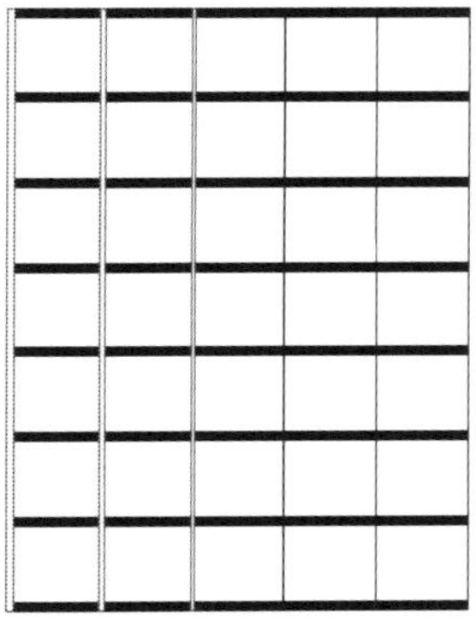
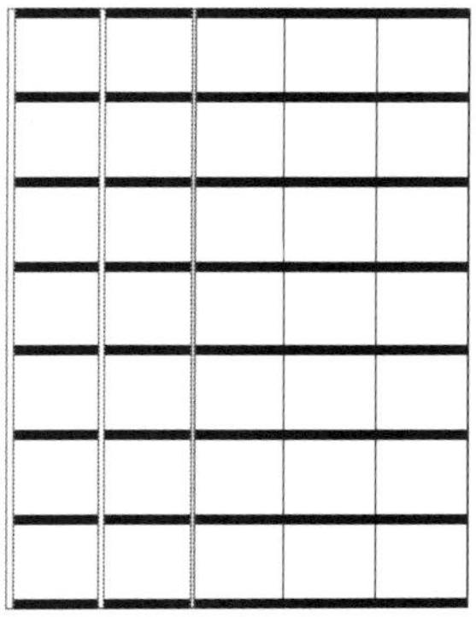
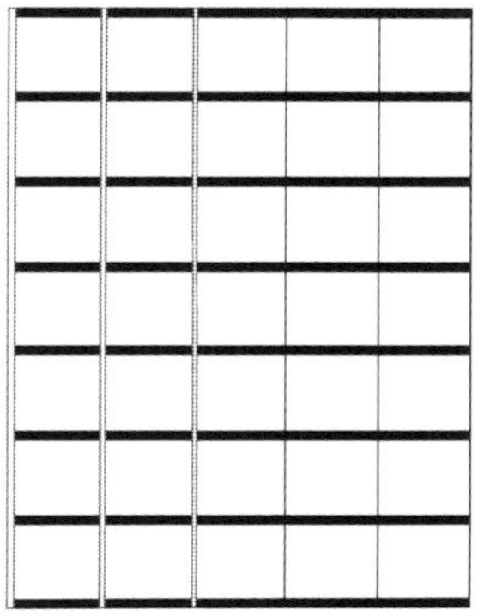
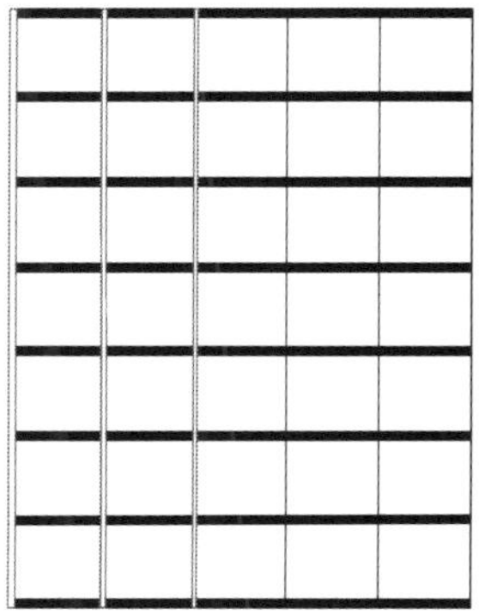
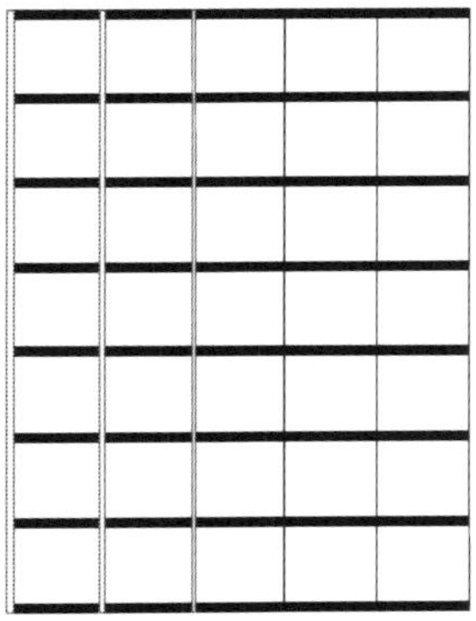
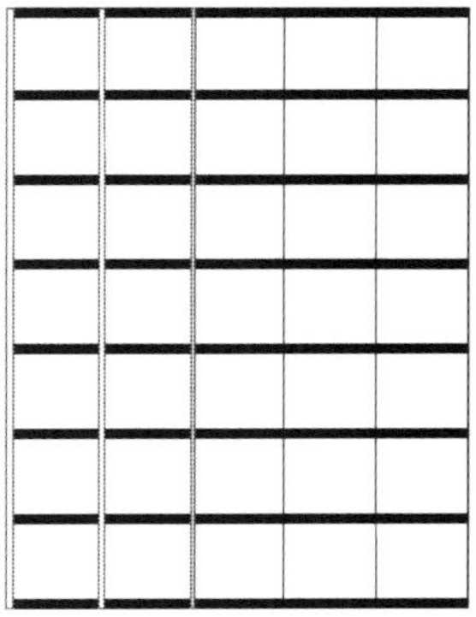
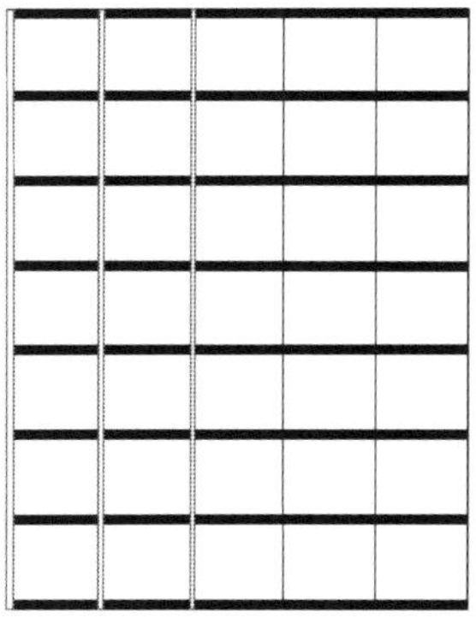
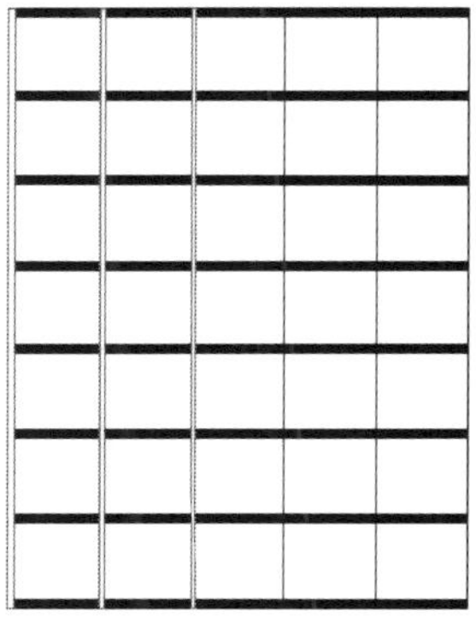
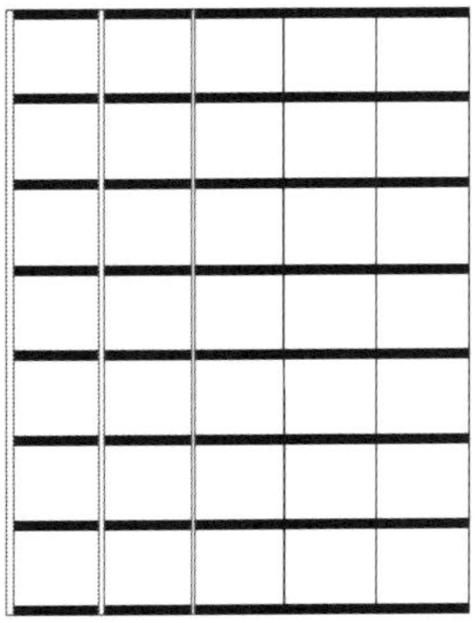
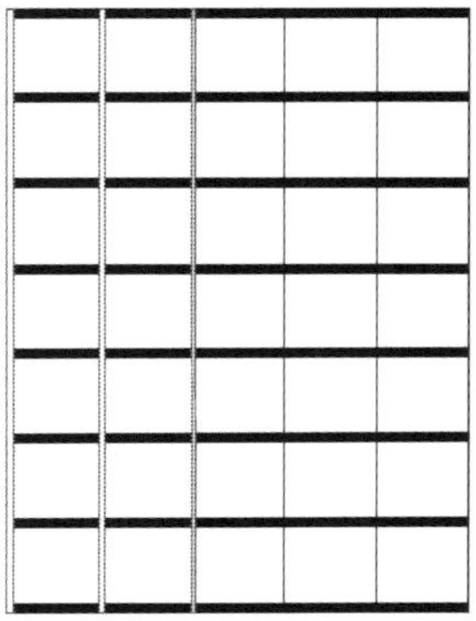
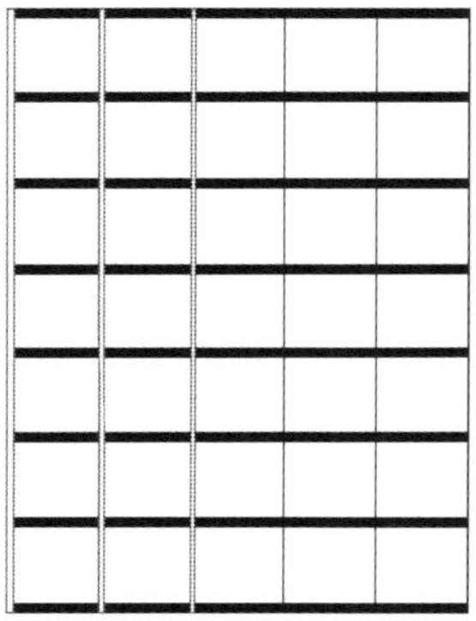
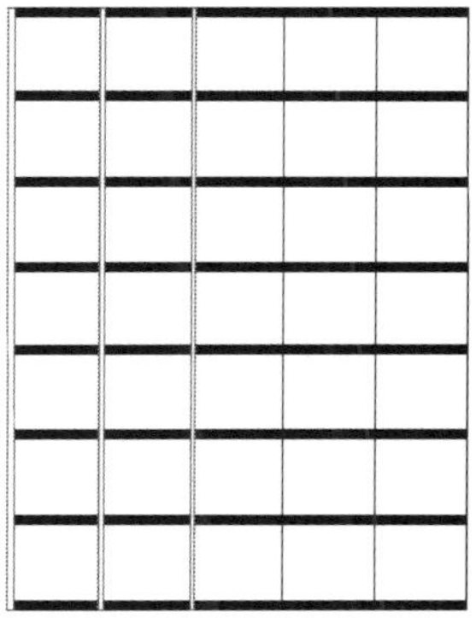

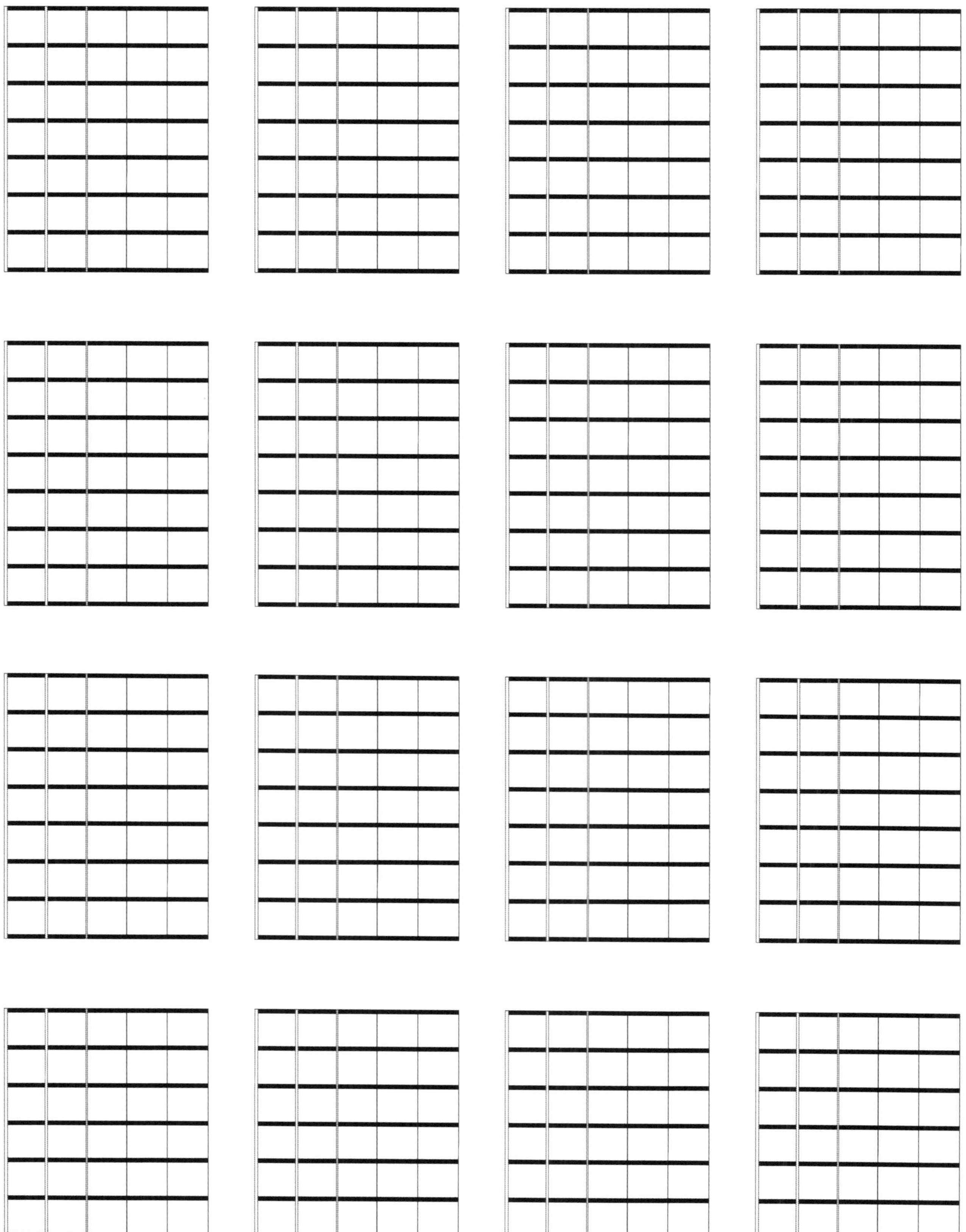

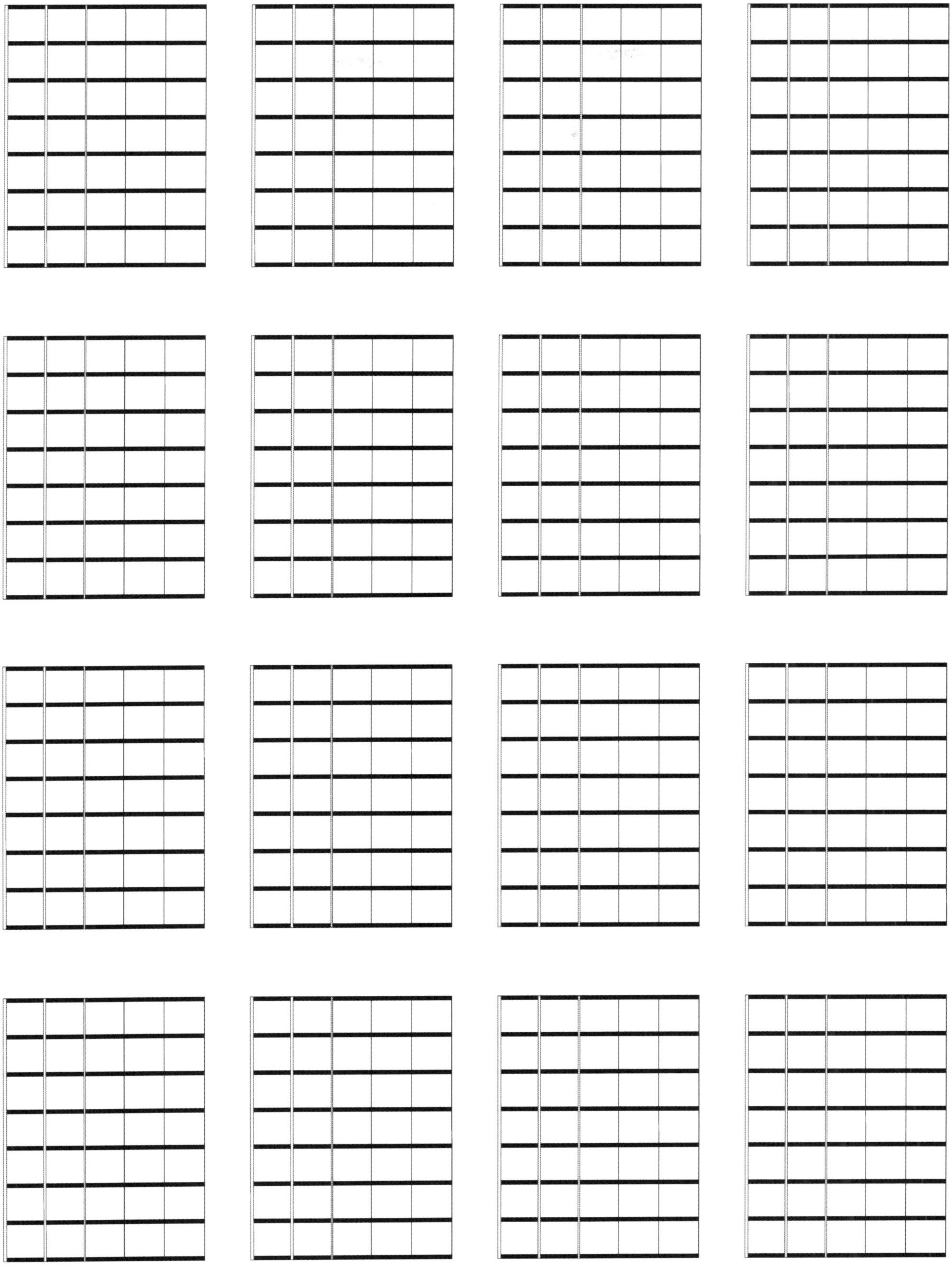

Guitar Books from Fundamental-Changes.Com

Fundamental Changes in Jazz Guitar I: The Major ii V I for Bebop Guitar

Minor ii V Mastery for Jazz Guitar

Jazz Blues Soloing for Guitar

Guitar Scales in Context

Drop 2 Chord Voicings for Jazz and Modern Guitar

The CAGED System and 100 Licks for Blues Guitar

The Complete Guide to Playing Blues Guitar Book One: Rhythm Guitar

The Complete Guide to Playing Blues Guitar Book Two: Melodic Phrasing

The Complete Guide to Playing Blues Guitar Book Three: Beyond Pentatonics

The Complete Guide to Playing Blues Guitar Compilation (Paperback)

The Complete Technique, Theory and Scales Compilation for Guitar (Paperback)

Sight Reading Mastery for Guitar

Complete Technique for Modern Guitar

Rock Guitar Un-CAGED: The CAGED System and 100 Licks for Rock Guitar

Jazz Guitar Chord Mastery

Be Social

Join over 4000 people getting six free guitar lessons each day on Facebook:

www.facebook.com/FundamentalChangesInGuitar

Keep up to date on Twitter

@Guitar_Joseph

8282841R00059

Printed in Germany
by Amazon Distribution
GmbH, Leipzig